AUSTRALASIAN ARTISTS AT THE FRENCH SALONS

REVISED AND UPDATED

Compiled by Tom Thompson

ETT IMPRINT

SYDNEY—PARIS LINK

This 3rd edition in colour with additional material published 2023

First published in 2019 by ETT Imprint, Exile Bay
Reprinted with additional material 2021

Compiled by Tom Thompson

Published in association with Pierre Sanchez
at Éditions de l'Échelle de Jacob, Dijon

Tea in the Salons originally published in *Les Peintres Britanniques dans les Salons Parisiens des origins à 1939* (L'echelle de Jacob, Dijon 2002)

ETT IMPRINT
PO Box R1906
Royal Exchange NSW 1225 Australia

ISBN 978-1-922698-95-7 (paper)
ISBN 978-1-922698-96-4 (ebook)

Design by Hanna Gotlieb and Tom Thompson
Cover: *Sur La Plage* by Ethel Carrick Fox, 1910

for Monique & Jean-Paul Delamotte

with abiding affection

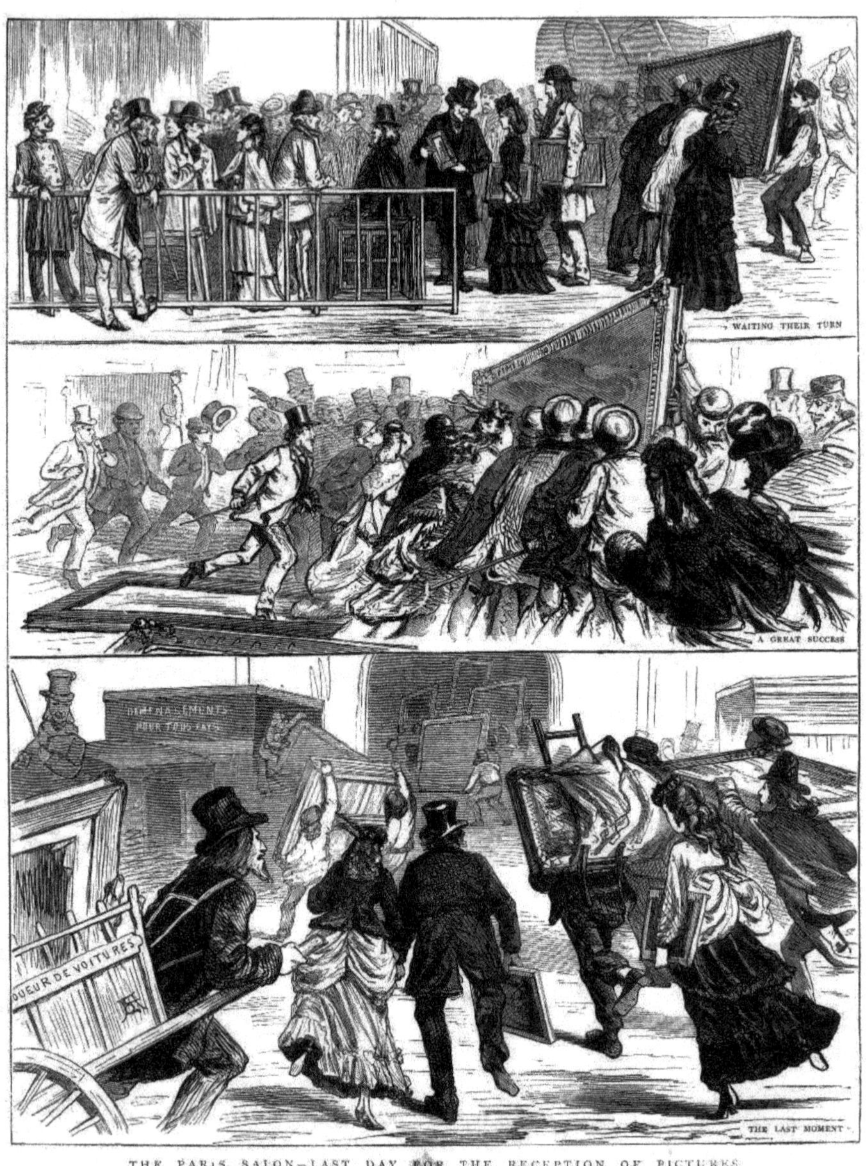

A page from *The Graphic*, April 20 1872.

CONTENTS

List of Exhibitions

AUTOMNE	Salon d'Automne
BORDEAUX	Salon des Amis des Arts and Ind. Bordelais
E.U.	Exposition Universelles
EXPOSITION DES XX	Les Vingt
Galerie Devambez	Influential private gallery
Galerie Georges Petit	Influential private gallery
GRAVEUR MODERNE AMERICAINE	Modern American engravings
HIVER	Salon d'Hiver
INDÉPENDANTS	Salon de la Société des Artistes Indépendants
LIBRE ESTHÉTIQUE	A successor of Les Vingt
LILLE	Union artistique du Nord de la France
NANTES	Salon de la Société des Amis des arts de Nantes
LYON	Salon de la Société Lyonnaise des Beaux-Arts
REIMS	Salon de la Société des Amis des arts de Reims
ROUEN	Salon de la Société des Amis des arts de Rouen
SAF	Salon de la Société des Artistes Français
SDAI	Salon de la Société des Artistes Indépendants
SALON DES PEINTRES ORIENTALISTS	Salon de la Société des Peintres Orientalists
SNBA	Salon de la Société National des Beaux Arts
SALON DES ARTISTES DÉCORATEURS	Salon de la Société des Artistes Décorateurs
TUILERIES	Salon des Tuileries
UNION DES FEMMES PEINTRES	A group promoting female artists
* Armory Shows Boston and New York	

PREFACE

The records in this book are surprising, revealing the extraordinary involvement of Australian and New Zealand artists who exhibited in the French Salons between 1872 and 1939. It is drawn from Beatrice Crespon-Halotier's much larger work, *Les Peintres Britanniques dans les Salons Parisiens des Origines à 1939,* produced by *Éditions de l'Echelle de Jacob* for the Louvre in 2002. This smaller, select edition focuses solely on artists from our region and includes new, unpublished material regarding their involvement in the French salons.

Apart from the attraction England had for Australian and New Zealand artists in the nineteenth and twentieth centuries, France, and in particular, Paris, was also a powerful magnet. During these years it became the art capital of the world, attracting artists from all over the globe. For Australians and New Zealanders, the journey was a greater feat than for most, given the enormous distance they had to travel. This, in turn, sometimes led to longer *soujourns* than their counterparts from closer geographic regions.

Many of these Antipodean artists lived and worked in France for lengthy periods of their lives. For some, the attraction was study at the famous art schools of Paris, principally in *La Grande Chaumiere,* Carolus Duran's studio and the *Académie Julian.* New Zealand artist, Frances Hodgkins even taught in Colarossi's *Académie* in Paris, the first woman to be appointed an instructor there. Many Australians, including Dorrit Black, Grace Crowley and Anne Danger, also studied at the Lhote Studio, an art school run by French artist, Andre Lhote. These schools allowed them to advance their art practice and try their luck in being accepted into the open salons of Paris and other regions of France.

Some of the best-known of these artists, like Rupert Bunny, lived much of his life in France, before returning to Australia. He spent close to half a century there and became a focal point and advisor for many of his countrymen and women, coming there for the first time. John Peter Russell left Australia and spent most of his life in France painting, interacting and influencing many eminent European artists, such as Matisse, as referenced by Hilary Spurling in her biography of Matisse. A large body of Russell's work was bequeathed to the Louvre and much of this work is now on permanent display at the *Musée des Beaux-Arts* at Morlaix in Brittany, not far from the artist's beloved *Belle Isle.* Russell finally returned to Australia and spent his later years here. Other coastal regions attracted other Australian artists, such as David Davies, a member of the Heidelberg School and painter of the iconic *Moonrise.* Davies lived at Dieppe, on the Normandy coast, for twenty-five years, running art classes and developing his own painting.

Indeed, there were numerous Australian and New Zealand artists who committed many years of their lives to France and undoubtedly left their mark on the art community and their chosen friends within French society. The desire to live in France and work there is still an attraction for artists today. These records of the open salons of France will assist in developing an invaluable tapestry of awareness of Australian and New Zealand artists who lived and worked there. It is an important reference book, long overdue, and will undoubtedly become a resource for researchers, art collectors and enthusiasts alike. I am delighted to see it and commend its Australian publisher, Tom Thompson, from ETT Imprint and his French counterpart, Pierre Sanchez, from *Éditions de l'Echelle de Jacob.* I must also mention, with thanks and affection, that indefatigable supporter of Australia in France, Jean Paul Delamotte, who first brought the original book to Tom's attention.

Daniel Pata

FOREWORD

Artists from Australia and New Zealand, such as those listed here, travelled to Europe in the late 19th and early 20th centuries to enhance skill and reputation through study in the Louvre and various academies of art. For many, the goal was to exhibit at the Paris Salons, and with this in mind, some became pupils of noted academicians, aware that an influential voice in the judging process was an asset to selection.

This text is drawn from *Les Peintres Britanniques dans les Salons Parisiens des Origines à 1939*, a scholarly work, complied by Béatrice Crespon-Halotier and published by L'Échelle de Jacob in 2002. But the focus of this smaller selection is solely antipodean artists and there are many additions and minor corrections, thanks to Pierre Sanchez and Tom Thompson.

Olivier Meslay's fascinating essay, *Tea in the Salons,* which accompanied the original text, is also included as an appendix. It describes the genesis of the original work, aspects of the Salons as they relate to French-Anglo exchanges and the larger context, wherein Australians and New Zealanders, as members of the British Commonwealth, were 'British' artists, an arena dominated by such artistic giants as Constable and Turner.

The earliest exhibitors listed here are celebrated names, like Mortimer Menpes (1882) and Rupert Bunny (1887) but there are less familiar artists, such as Edward Levy Montefiore, who exhibited throughout the 1870s. Waves of hopeful aspirants followed, some renowned in their home country; many with reputations still to make.

So, what did it mean to exhibit at one of the Paris Salons in the late 19th and early 20th centuries and how were these Salons constituted?

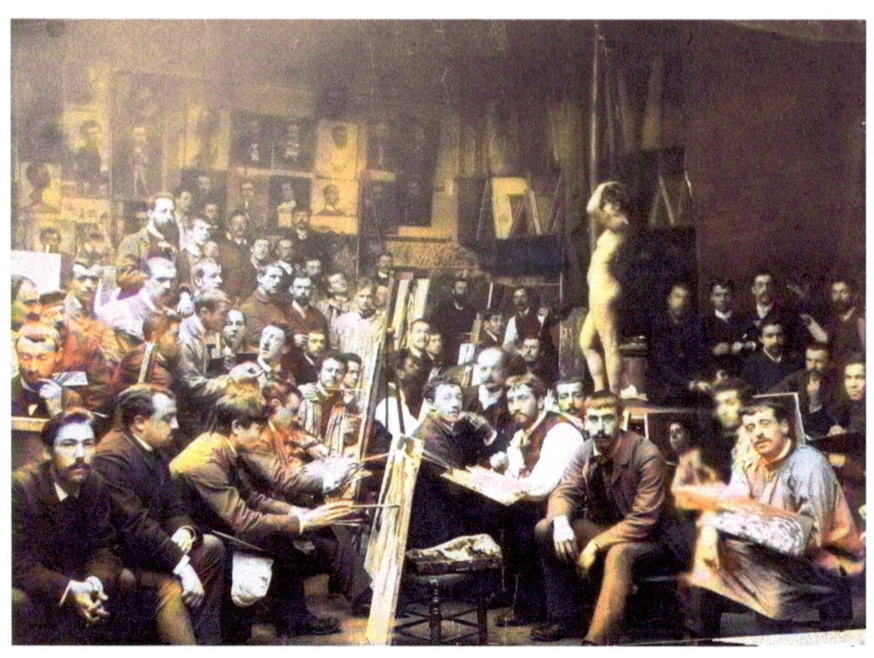

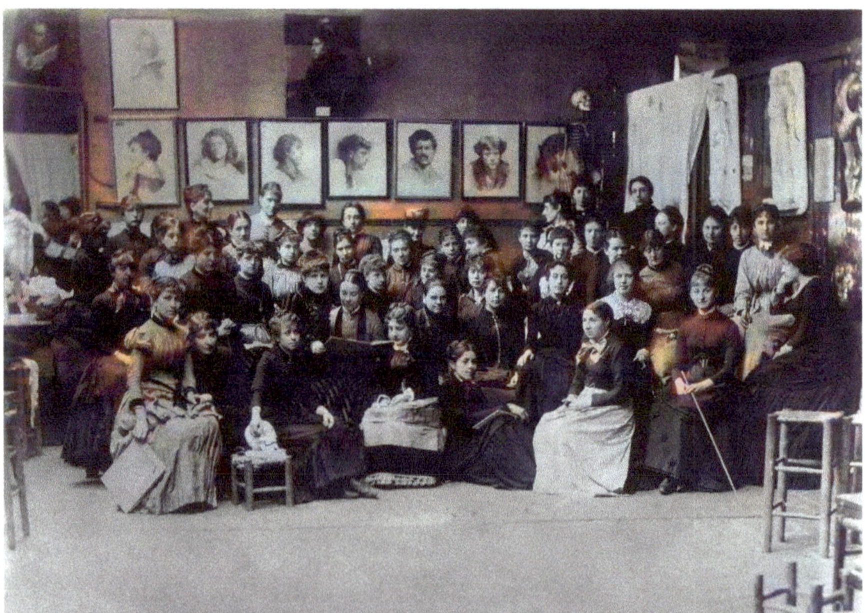

(Top) Painters at the Academie Julian 1884;
(Lower)Women artists at the Academie Julian, Paris 1886.

The hundreds of entries listed under Rupert Bunny's name from 1887-1932 hint at the scope of different exhibitions and the Salons they represented. His work was variously selected by the *Société des Artistes Français* (SAF), the *Expositions Universelles* (E.U.), the *Société Nationale des Beaux-Arts* (SNBA), the Salons of Nantes, Lille and Bordeaux, the *Salon d'Automne*, and the *Galerie Georges Petit* and *Galerie Devambez.* The Parisian Salons were linked to some of the most influential figures in French art in that period, while the regional Salons were linked to organisations like *Amis des Arts* and *Ind. Bordelais* (Bordeaux); *Société des Amis des arts de Nantes* (Nantes); and *Union artistique du Nord de la France* (Lille).

Apart from these, there were Salons where Bunny did not exhibit but others from our region did. Among these were the *Salon des Indépendants* of the *Société des Artistes Indépendants* (SDAI), *Exposition des XX, Libre Esthetique, Société des Peintres Orientalistes, Salon d'Hiver, Société des Artistes Décorateurs, Salon de la Société Lyonnaise des Beaux-Arts* (Lyon), *Salon des Tuileries,* and the *Union des Femmes Peintres.*

In the 19th century, before internecine disputes led to the establishment of smaller Salons, the annual or biannual Salon exhibition was the cultural event of the year in France[1]. During the 1860s, and throughout the period of change described here, artists' submissions were vetted by the Salon jury, who favoured academic work, painted within academic conventions. Innovation was discouraged and to a large degree scorned. The American artist, Mary Cassatt, for example, found that her work had been accepted when she applied the dark background required by the jury but when she lightened it to a much higher key, the same work was rejected. This dissent over the conservatism of the jury increased and led to the first Impressionist exhibition in 1874.

Artists like Cassatt and the other Impressionists were incensed by the system of judging and awarding medals and prizes and made it a condition that anyone who showed at the Impressionist exhibitions could not submit work to the 'official' Salon.

The composition of the 'official' Salon jury also changed over time, which in turn influenced who was selected for exhibition and the liberality with which works were accepted. It has been said, for example, that in some years, acceptance of work by foreign artists was sometimes a deliberate strategy, to encourage the sale of works outside France.

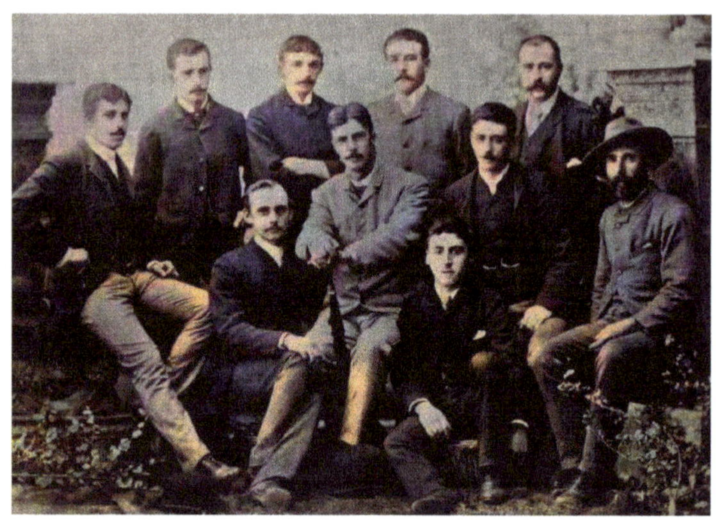

National Art School Students 1887:(from left, standing) J. Llewellyn Jones, Alexander Colquhoun, E. Phillips Fox, Frederick McCubbin. Seated: John Longstaff, Tudor St. George Tucker, J.J. Gibbs, A. Alston, David Davies, Fred Williams.

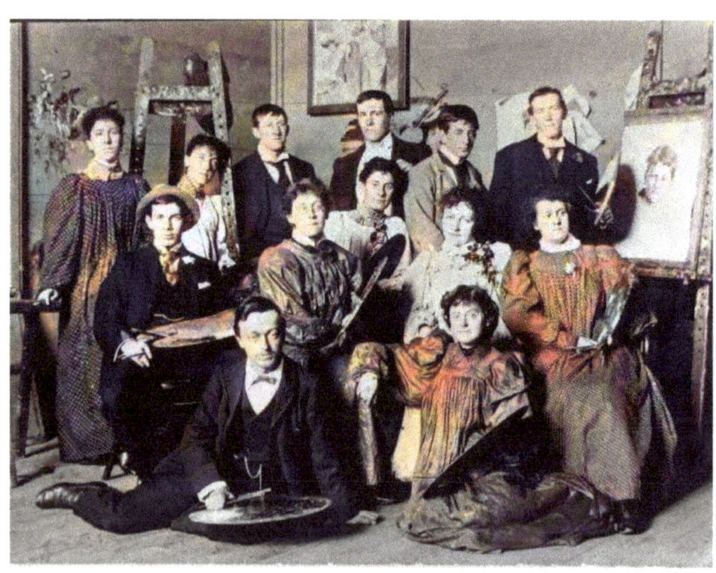

Students at the National Art Gallery School, Melbourne 1896. Back row: Amy Mann, Alice Kirkwood, Leon Pole George Coates, Albert Anes, Hugh Ramsey. Middle Row: James Macdonald, Dora Meeson, Jo Sweatman, Portia Geach, Isobel Hunter. Front row: George Pontin, Ada Coutie.

When the Impressionists established their rival but infinitely smaller exhibition, it was held at the same time as the 'official' Salon but, initially, the scale of the exhibition was matched by its lack of influence. Their persistence in staging eight exhibitions from 1874 to 1886 went hand-in-hand with broader social changes and the growing acceptance of more innovative work. Increasingly, this innovative work depicted scenes from everyday life, rather than the lofty historical, biblical and mythological themes favoured by the 'official' Salon.

Other factors were also in play. As one among many responses to complaints about conservatism, the Salon jury opened its doors to over 7,000 submissions in 1880, making the event difficult to manage. This proliferation led to an end to official State support and the beginning of control of the Salon by an artist-led organisation, the *Société des Artistes Français* or SAF.

In 1884, an alternative exhibition, the *Salon des Indépendants,* was instituted by the *Société des Artistes Indépendants* but unlike the SAF exhibition, there was no jury and no prices. Alongside these developments, art dealers, such as George Petit, also began to stage important exhibitions for artists who were considered innovative, either as part of international expositions or as one artist shows.

This tide of change continued and in 1890 a group of artists separated from SAF and formed their own *Société Nationale des Beaux-Arts* or SNBA, which held a competing annual Salon, known as the *Salon des Champs de Mars.* However, both the SAF and SNBA were still considered conventional and from the point of view of critics, "dull"[2]. So, in spite of their dominance, the official Salons were losing their authority in these years and were no longer a guarantee of success, either financially or in terms of reputation.

The State made acquisitions at all these Salons, as well as the *Salon des Indépendants,* and the *Salon d'Automne,* which was created in 1903 to exhibit the most innovative works[3]. In the years leading up to World War 1, however, some of the more influential dealers, such as Daniel-Henri Kahnweiler, were advising their artists not to bother submitting to the Salons because they no longer held the *cachet* they once had and were "a waste of time"[4].

This was, doubtless, the right advice for artists like Picasso and Braque, whom Kahnweiler represented, but it was less salient for the many others whose art practice was still steeped in 19th century and later, Impressionist and Post-Impressionist traditions.

Paris 17 Rue Guillaume-Tell XVIIe

Cher Monsieur

Voici les renseignements demandés, concernant Mademoiselle Davidson dont les prénoms sont: Elène. Bessie ~~Davidson~~ ou Bessie Elène.

Née à Adélaïde (Australie du Sud) le 22 Mai 1880, elle est sujet Britannique.

Besnard.

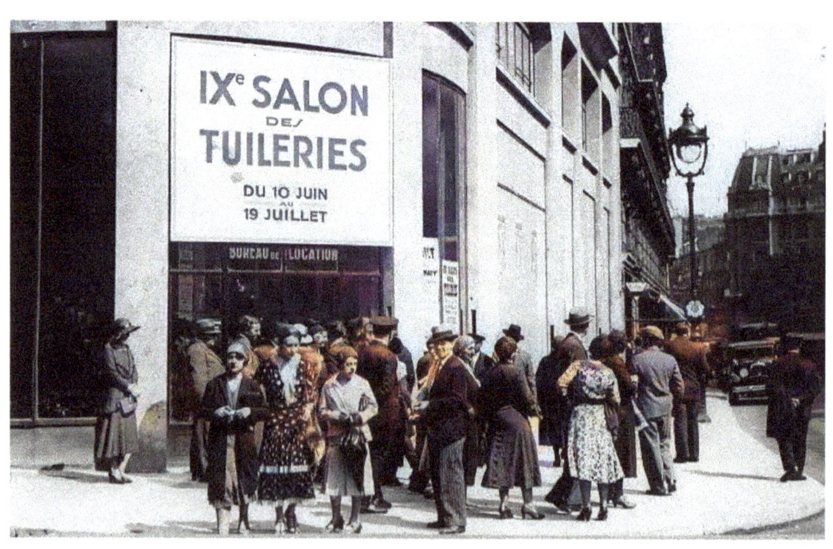

(Top) A letter of support from Albert Besnard regarding Bessie Davidson and her showing at the Salon des Tuileries; (Lower) Crowds wait for the opening of the Salon des Tuileries, Paris 1931.

Artists like Rupert Bunny appear to have weathered the changing nature of the Salons, with works submitted up to 1932. And, a host of others from Australia and New Zealand still saw exhibition at the Salons as one of their primary goals. This included artists such as Margaret Preston, later regarded as an early Australian modernist, who fought for selection in the early 20th century and who was exhibited on four occasions between 1905 and 1914.

Preston returned to Australia at the end of World War 1 and forged her own path in creating what she styled as a national art form. At the same time, her close friend, Bessie Davidson, remained in Paris and remained committed to the Salon process, exhibiting more than one hundred works up to 1939. But her commitment did not extend to continuing support for the more official Salons and in 1923, Davidson was one of the founding members of the *Salon des Tuileries*, created by friends and fellow artists such as Albert Besnard and Antoine Bourdelle, as an alternative to the *Salon National des Beaux Arts*, the *Salon d'Automne* and the *Salon des Indépendants*[5].

The newer Salons that developed also approached the hanging of works in a very different manner. When submissions to the official Salons had reached such large numbers, works were hung from floor to ceiling, with the number of votes received by a work helping to determine its position. Only works which had received a unanimous, or near unanimous vote, were hung 'on the line', where they could be seen and enjoyed by the crowds who visited. Being 'skyed', or hung very high up, was a sign of insignificance and works became larger in an attempt to gain attention[6].

The Impressionists, with limited works to manage, were able to hang them more equitably and dealers such as George Petit, when he came to stage exhibitions, often hung works in the Japanese manner, in a single line. These exhibitions became more private and exclusive and not the mass-visitations that had once thronged to the older Salons, where a quarter of a million people and more came to see, and be seen. The private showings at private galleries were harbingers of how the art market was to develop in the 20th century, when an influential dealer became the goal of most artists, rather than acceptance at a public exhibition.

It is hoped that these very general notes will allow readers to better enjoy the wonderful details given in this book for each entry; not just artist and title, but often medium, exhibition number, price, the artist's address in

Paris or England, and additional biographical details, where available. The Salon acronyms that appear alongside their names may also suggest their allegiances and help readers to appreciate the process of selection to which they were subjected and the character of the Salon in which they exhibited.

Finally, it is hoped that the many lesser known names here will stimulate further research to enhance understanding of how artists from Australia and New Zealand saw themselves on these international platforms and the many lessons they brought back to their home countries.

Elizabeth Butel, March 2019

1. Delacour, H. and Leca, B., 2011, 'The Decline and Fall of the Paris Salon: a Study in the Deinstitutionalisation Process of a Field Configuring Event in the Cultural Activities', M@n@gement, Vol. 14, pp. 436-466

2. Delacour, H. and Leca, B., 2011, 'The Decline and Fall of the Paris Salon: a Study in the Deinstitutionalisation Process of a Field Configuring Event in the Cultural Activities,' M@n@gement, Vol. 14, pp. 436-466

3. Meslay, O, 2002, 'Tea in the Salons' reprinted herein. This list of purchases includes two Australians, Rupert Bunny in 1904, and E. Phillips Fox in 1906 (ref. page 126)

4. Delacour, H. and Leca, B., 2011, 'The Decline and Fall of the Paris Salon: a Study in the Deinstitutionalisation Process of a Field Configuring Event in the Cultural Activities,' M@n@gement, Vol. 14, pp. 436-466

5. Little, P., 2003, A Studio in Montparnasse, Craftsman House, Melbourne, Australia, p. 94.

6. Milner, J., 1988, The Studios of Paris, the Capital of Art in the Late Nineteenth Century, Yale University Press, New Haven and London, p. 51.

A

ABBOTT Inez
Born Bendigo, Victoria, Australia
16 rue de la Grande-Chaumière, chez M. Castelucho, Paris (14th)
1932 – (SNBA) 2 - Étude (aquarelle)
ADAM Edith Constance Me
Born Oamaru, New Zealand
16 rue de la Grande-Chaumière, Paris (14th)
1924 – (INDEPENDANTS) 7 - Tête de jeune fille (sculpture) (800 fr)
8 - L'esclave (sculpture) (1000 fr)
ADET Emile or Adrien Emile
Born 1868 Melbourne or Sydney, Australia.
Amis des arts. 51e expo. Elève de Gumery (Paris), 189 rue de Saint-Genès, Bourdeaux
1903 – (BORDEAUX) 2 - Printemps : environs de Paris.
3 - Sous bois.
Amis des arts. 54e expo. Elève de M. Adolphe Gumery.
A Paris-Auteuil, 23 rue Poussin, Paris (16th)
1906 – (BORDEAUX) 3 - Environs de Saint-Servan (Ille-et-Vilaine)
Amis des arts. 72e expo. Elève de Gumery et Ad. Gaussen.
A Marseille, rue Venture. Paris (10th)
1928 – (BORDEAUX) 6 - Châtaigniers, château des Leszes (750 fr)
ALISON-GREENE Anne Eliza a.k.a. Annie Green
Born 27 September 1878 Dorset, G.B., died 2 July 1954 at Wynnum, Queensland.
143 boulevard Saint-Michel, Paris (5th)
1913 – (SAF) 831 - Étude.
832 - Etude.
8 bis, rue Campagne-Première, Paris (14th)
1914 – (SAF) 936 – 'Marie'.
15 rue Campagne-Première, Paris (14th)
1920 – (SAF) 15 - La vieille bonne.

	16 - La petite Elise.
	17 - Bateaux de pêche.
1921 – (SNBA)	14 - Portrait.
	15 - Le Port.
	16 - Portrait 'Elise'.
1923 – (SNBA)	12 - Portait de Mme N...
	13 - Portrait.
	14 - Portrait.
1924 – (SNBA)	17 - Portrait.
	18 - Mme C...
1925 – (SNBA)	7 - Portrait.
1926 – (SNBA)	16 - Portrait (Mme J.).
	17 - Portrait.
1927 – (SNBA)	14 - Portrait de Mme C...
	15 - Portrait de Nellie.
1928 – (SNBA)	34 - Mademoiselle C...
1929 – (SNBA)	39 - Mlle V...
	40 - Mme S...
1930 – (SNBA)	51 - Jania Nepo.
1931 – (SNBA)	49 - Nina.
	50 - Valentine.
	51 - Portrait.
	52 - Portrait.
1932 – (SNBA)	45 - Portrait.
	46 - Portrait.
1933 – (SNBA)	31 - Portrait.
1934 – (SNBA)	26 - Portrait.
	27 - Etude.
1935 – (SNBA)	30 - Mlle L...
	31 - Lydie.
	32 - Etude.
1939 – (SNBA)	7 - Portrait.
	8 - Etude.

ALTSON, Abbey or Aby
Born 21 August 1864 Middlesbrough-on-Tees, G.B., died 7 November 1948 New York, USA.

Elève de M. Blanc. 2 rue d'Odessa, 2 hôtel Saint-Mal, Paris (14th)

1892 – (SAF) 9 - Echo,
10 - Rita

Elève de M. Folingsby. 2 rue d'Odessa, Paris (14th)

1893 – (SAF) 16 - *L'âge d'or* (mention honorable)

Elève de M. Folingsby, 2 Queen Road Studios,
Saint John's Wood, London G.B.

1896 – (SAF) 27 - *Portrait.*

ASHTON Will or John William
Born 1881 Clifton, York, England, died 1963 Mosman, NSW Australia.

15 quai Voltaire, The American Art C°, Paris (7th)

1904 – (SAF) 44 - Beau jour d'hiver.

125 boulevard du Montparnasse, Paris (6th)

1906 – (SAF) 51 - Marine : - Cornouailles.
52 - Le marais.

Stanley St. North Adelaide,
Australia & 65 boulevard Arago, Paris (13th)

1912 – (SNBA) 43 - La mer le soir.

Connaught Club, London, G.B.

1913 – (SAF) 43 - Le soir, sur les côtes de Cornouaille.
44 - Port Victor (Australie méridionale).

125 boulevard du Montparnasse,
The Paris American Art C°, Paris (6th)

1914 – (SAF) 50 - Pont Louis-Philippe.
51 - Un quai à Paris.

B

BAKER-CLACK Arthur

Born 1877 Boolaroo, Australia, died 1955 Folkestone, England

11 rue Vavin, Paris (6th)

1913 – (INDEPENDANTS) 147 - Fleurs (sur fond oriental).

148 - Singe et tambour (coin de nursery).

149 - Pierrette.

BAKER Christina Asquith

Born 1869 London, Australian citizen, died 1960

Elève de MM. Baschet et Schommer. 15 quai Voltaire, The American Art C° Paris (7th)

1904 – (SAF) 68 - Portrait de Mlle A.M. P...

69 - La liseuse.

BARKER Mlle Caroline

Born 1894 Melbourne, Australia

29 Broadhurst Gardens, London, G.B.

1926 – (SAF) 104 - Delphiniums.

BIRLEY Oswald Hornby Joseph

Born 1880 Auckland, New Zealand, died 1952 London

Elève de M. Marcel. Baschet et Schommer. 63 rue de Seine, Paris (6th)

1901 – (SAF) 199 - Portrait de dame en noir.

200 - Portrait d'un jeune homme.

1902 – (SAF) 151 - Étude de femme.

152 - Portrait.

Elève de M. Baschet. 6 rue de Furstenberg, Paris (6th)

1903 – (SAF) 165 - Portrait du docteur J. Gowing-Middleton M.D. (mention honorable)

166 - Etude de nu.

Elève de M. Baschet. 6 Rue de Furstenberg Paris (6th)

1904 – (SAF) 173 - Étude de nu.

174 - Portrait de Mme R. C... et sa fille.

Elève de M. Baschet. 4 Sackville Street, London, G.B.

1905 – (SAF) 177 - Portrait de Mme ***.

178 - Portrait de John Craig, Esquire.

Elève de M. Baschet. 48 Grove End Road, Saint John's Wood, London, G.B.

1906 – (SAF) 170 - Portrait de Mme W...
171 - La trieuse de chiffons.

Elève de M. Baschet. 48 Grove End Road, St John's Wood, London, G.B.

1907 – (SAF) 167 - Portrait d'enfants.
168 - Portrait de Mme G. A...

1908 – (SAF) 163 - Sir George Armstrong, baronnet.

1909 – (SAF) 177 - La robe jaune. (illustration)
(médaille 3ème classe)

Elève de M. Baschet. 48 Grove End Road. St John's Wood, London, G.B.

1910 – (SAF) 201 - Les deux frères.
202 – 'L'Apache' (Miss Béatrice Collier)

1911 – (SAF) 171 - La loge.

1912 – (SAF) 176 - Le châle chinois.

1913 – (SAF) 172 - Femme en rose et noir.

1920 – (SAF) 161 - Portrait d'un officier italien.

1921 – (SAF) 193 - Sem.

1922 – (SAF) 185 - M. Lucien Guitry.

62 Wellington Road, London, G.B.

1931 – (SAF) 240 - The Dowager Countess of Airlie.

1932 – (SAF) 254 - Danseuse royale, Bangkok.

BLASHKI Miles Evergood

Born 1871 Melbourne, Victoria, died 1939 Melbourne

Amberley, Sussex, G.B.

1914 – (SAF) 206 - Vallée d'Arun.

BOWEN Stella or Estelle or Esther Gwendolyn Born 1893 Adelaide, South Australia, died 1947 London

Chez Mme Oliver Max. Hueffer, 65 boulevard Arago, Paris (13th)

1923 – (AUTOMNE) 216 - Portrait de H. J. Birnstingl, Esq.

217 - Portrait de M. N. Galmar.
218 - Portrait de Ford Madox Ford, Esq.

65 boulevard Arago, Paris (13th).

1924 – (TUILERIES) 217 - Villefranche.

Guermantes, près Lagny, chez M. Ford, Seine-et-Marne, France.

1925 – (SNBA) 53 - Portrait de Mme Serruys.

84 rue Notre-Dame-des-Champs, Paris (6th)

1927 – (AUTOMNE) 268 - Tryptique.
269 - Portrait.

1929 – (AUTOMNE) 183 - Bouquet.

18 rue Boissonade, Paris (14th)

1931 – (AUTOMNE) 227 - Soleils.
228 - *Intérieur.*

BOWMAN Myril Mc Dougall or **BOWMAN-LLOYD** Myril

Born 1895 Sydney, Australia

Bowman Myrill Mc Dougall. 29 rue Campagne-Première, Paris (14th)

1925 – (TUILERIES) 201 (s) - David (bronze)

Lloyd Myril Bowman, 9 rue Campagne-Première, Paris (14th)

1926 – (TUILERIES) 1296 (s) - Eve (bronze, cire perdue).

Bowman-Lloyd Myril. Atelier 24 bis, 9 rue Campagne-Première, Paris (14th)

1927 – (TUILERIES) 298 (s) - La Guirlandière (bronze)

Bowman-Lloyd Myril. 9 rue Campagne-Première, Paris (14th)

1928 – (TUILERIES) 375 - Femme assise (bronze)
376 - Tête de Sainte Jeanne (bronze)

Lloyd M. Atelier, 24 bis, 9 rue Campagne-Première, Paris (14th)

1929 – (TUILERIES) 817 (s) - Torse d'une femme.

BOXALL Arthur d'Auvergne

Born 1895 Port Elliot, Australia, died 1944 Adelaide, Australia

14 Clifton Road, London, G.B.

1928 – (SAF) 281 - Winter in London.

BROCKES Mlle May

Born Melbourne, Australia

43 boulevard des Capucines, Lloyds National Provincial and Foreign Bank, Paris (2nd)

1933 – (SDAI) 745 - Peinture.
746 - Peinture.
747 - Peinture.

BROOKE Edmund Walpole

Born Melbourne, Australia.

Elève de MM. Bouguereau, T. Robert-Fleury et Gérôme, 16 rue de la Grande-Chaumière, Paris (14th)

1891 – (SAF) 240 - Aux champs.

BROOKES May

Born Australia.

Galerie Georges Petit. Exposition May Brookes. Fleurs sauvages d'Australie. 17-31 décembre 1932.

1932 –

1 - Gommier rouge. Bottle Brush et Perroquets.
2 - Waratah. Sydney N. S. W. et Pointsettias, Queensland.
3 - Gommier rouge. Victoria.
4 - Oiseau lyre. Victoria.
5 - Oiseau lyre. Victoria.
6 - Gommier rouge.
7 - Sturt's Pea (Sud Australie) et Patte de Kangourou (plante).
8 - Fleurs sauvages.
9 - Pare-feu.
10 - Orchidées bleues, Lotus bleus, Lys.
11 - Orchidées, Heats, Sturt's Pea.
12 - Lys verts. Queensland.
13 - Fleurs sauvages.
14 - Waratah (New South Wales).
15 - Pointsettia. Queensland.
16 - Oiseau Kokaburra. Australie.
17 - Cocatoo. Australie.

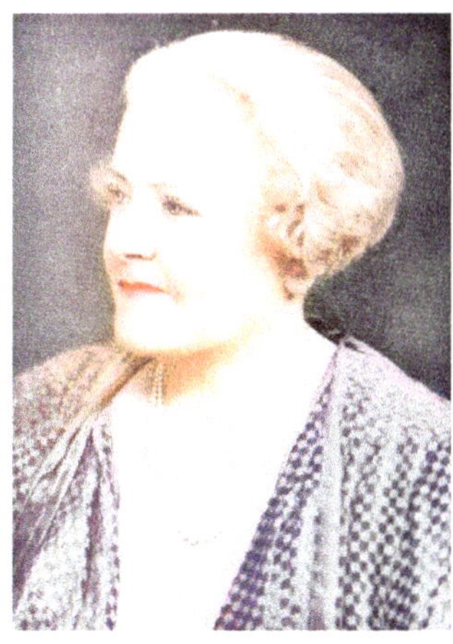

May Brookes

18 - Mont Macedon. Victoria (aquarelle)

19 - Mont Macedon. Victoria (painting in oil)

20 - Bottle Brush.

21 - Paravent (painting in oil)

22 - Lys roses (aquarelle)

23 - Lys tigrés (aquarelle)

24 - Gloxinias (aquarelle)

25 - Gloxinias (aquarelle)

26 - Orchidées (aquarelle sur soie).

27 - Magnolias dans un vase (aquarelle)

28 - Delphiniums (aquarelle)

29 - Tulipes et Narcisses. Hollande.

PAYSAGES

30 - Fjord et glacier de Norvège (aquarelle)

31 - Gorges du Vésubie (Alpes-Maritimes).

32 - Gorges du Vésubie (Alpes-Maritimes).

33 - Sospel (Alpes-Maritimes).

34 - Printemps, forêt de Saint-Germain (aquarelle)

35 - Automne, forêt de Saint-Germain (aquarelle)

36 - Gommiers au Cap Ferrat.

37 - Clochettes bleues et Chênes. Grande-Bretagne.

38 - Tulipes. Hollande.

39 - Tulipes. Hollande.

40 - Sur la route. Nice.

VITRINE - PORCELAINES

41 - Grand vase vert. Lézard Australien au grand col et oiseau Kokaburra.

	42 - Vase noir et or. Fleurs sauvages d'Australie.
	43 - Kolah Bear.
	44 - Cygnes et Gommiers.
	45 - Oiseau Kokaburra.
	46 - Kangourou.
	47 - Perroquets.
	48 - Jardinière bleue, lys, lotus.

BROOKS Ivan Wilkie

Born 1891 Melbourne, Australia, died 1952

Hôtel de la Haute-Savoie, boulevard Raspail, Paris (14th)

1921 – (AUTOMNE)	290 - Paysage.
	291 - Les Gerbes de paille.
	292 - Paysage.
	293 - Paysage, Chartres.

Hôtel Terminus, Dieppe, Pas-de-Calais, France

1922 – (AUTOMNE)	297 - Dieppe, le quai Henri-IV.
	298 - La Fenêtre.
	299 - Nature morte, fleurs.
	300 - Truite saumonée.
	301 - Légumes et choses.
	302 - Maquereaux.
	303 - Vivres et robinette.

5 Kensington Park Gardens, London G.B.

1923 – (AUTOMNE)	239 - Dieppe en hiver (1000 fr)

Saint Olave's Priory, Yarmouth, G.B.

1924 – (AUTOMNE)	247 - Auberge anglaise.

BRYANT Annie

Born 1874 Port Adelaide, South Australia.

The Rectory, Cloyst Saint-Lawrence, near Exeter, Devon, G.B.

1925 – (SAF)	113 - Golden Glow.
1931 – (SAF)	360 - By the Roan in Devon.
	361 - Sunset.
1932 – (SAF)	378 - Sussex (illustration)
1933 – (SAF)	355 - Sunset after rain (illustration)
1934 – (SNBA)	267 - By the Brook Peter Favy.

1934 – (SAF) 376 - Early spring.

1938 – (SAF) 268 - Winding River.

269 - Countess Weir.

1939 – (SAF) 444 - Evening Glow.

BRYANT Charles David Jones

Born 1883 Sydney, Australia, died 1937 Sydney

Elève de M. Julius Olsson – London, G.B.

1913 –(SAF) 282 - Brouillard du matin : Saint-Yves, Cornwall (mention honorable)

Chelsea Art Center, 143 Church Street, London G.B.

1932 – (SAF) 379 - Le Louvre.

BUCKLAND-WRIGHT John

Born 3 December 1897 Dunedin, New Zealand, died 27 September 1954 London, G.B.

97 rue Compans, Paris (19th)

1931 – (AUTOMNE) 264-265 (A) - Illustrations pour *L'Apocalypse.*

1932 – (AUTOMNE) 228 - Paysage.

229 - Fleurs.

1797 (section livres) - Illustration pour *L'Apocalypse,* de Saint Jean.

1798 (section livres) - Ditto.

1799 (section livres) - Hors-texte pour *Le Bibliophile.*

Ind. Bordelais. 8e année. 13 oct. – 11 nov. 1935. Sect. Peinture.

9 bis, rue de Valence (5th)

1935 – (BORDEAUX) 70 - Léda (gravure)

71 - Torse (gravure)

72 - Baigneuse et Satyre.

73 - Plage (wood)

Ind. Bordelais. 9e année. 18 oct. – 15 nov. 1936. Sect. Peinture.

9 bis, rue de Valence (5th)

1936 – (BORDEAUX) 101 - Artiste et Modèle (wood) (100 fr)

102 - Le Modèle (wood) (100 fr)
103 - Baigneuse et Satyre n°2 (gravure) (100 fr)
104 - Léda (wood) (100 fr)

BUNNY Rupert Charles Wulsten

Born 29 September 1864 Melbourne, Victoria, died 25 May 1947 Melbourne

Elève de MM. J.-P. Laurens et Léon Glaize. 2 Rue d'Odessa, Paris (14th)

1887 – (SAF) 2673 - Une nuit de Valpurgis (design)

Elève de MM. J.-P. Laurens et L. Glaize. 86 rue Notre-Dame-des-Champs, Paris (6th)

1888 – (SAF) 429 - Un sabbat.

1889 – (SAF) 413 - Sainte Cécile.

1890 – (SAF) 395 – Pastorale.
394 – Tritons (mention honorable)

Elève de MM. J.-P. Laurens, Benjamin-Constant et Léon Glaize. 18 bis, impasse du Maine, Paris (14th)

1892 – (SAF) 311 - Les roses de Sainte-Dorothée.

1893 – (SAF) 295 - Pastorale.

Elève de MM. J.-P. Laurens et Léon Glaize. 18 bis, Impasse du Maine, Paris (14th)

1894 – (SAF) 326 - Avant l'orage.
1988 - La toilette (pastel)

59 avenue de Saxe, Paris (7th)

1895 – (SAF) 327 - Le retour du jardin.
328 - Portrait de Mlle M...

1896 – (SAF) 347 - Portrait de M. P...
348 - Eos.

1897 – (SAF) 282 - Dolce farniente.
3563 - Embroidery (in collaboration with M. Besancenot)
3564 - Flora (embroidery)

1898 – (SAF) 339 - Au bord de la mer.
340 - 'La Penserosa'.

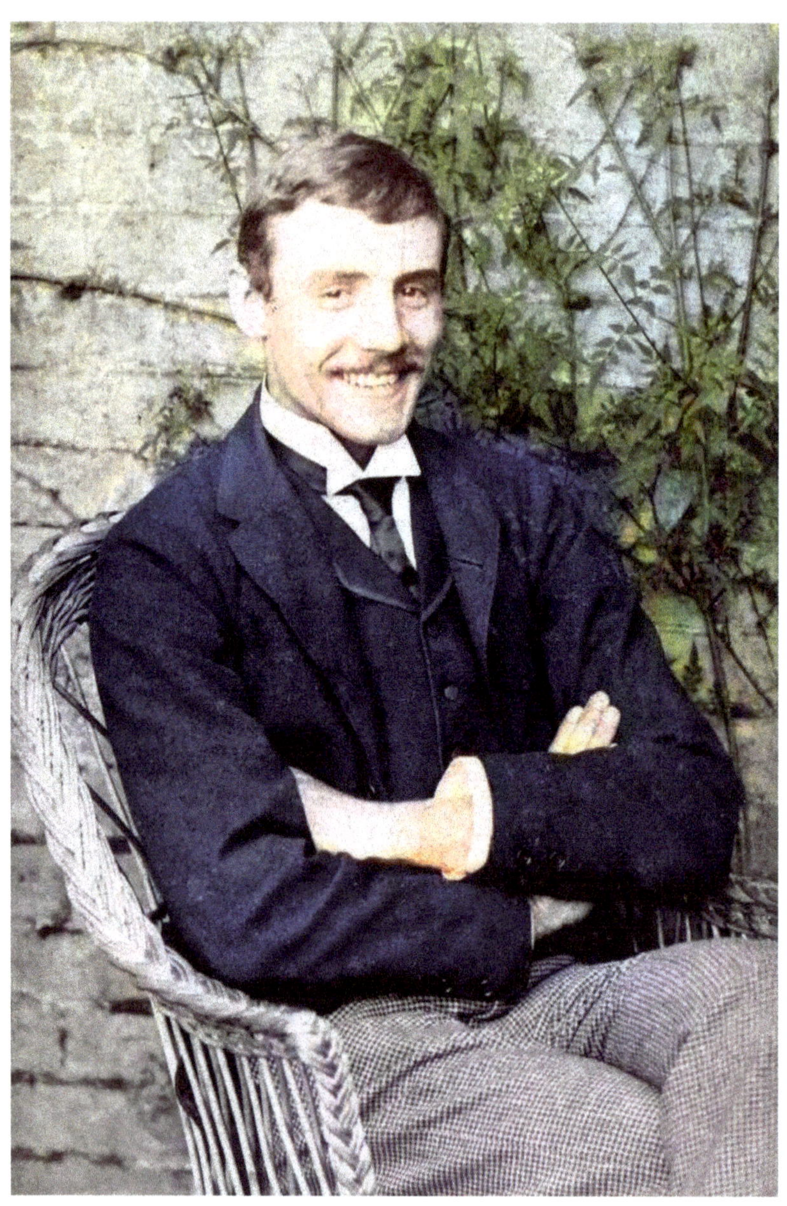

Rupert Bunny in Provence, 1884.

1899 – (SAF) 321 - Descente de croix.
322 - Enterrement de Ste Catherine à Alexandrie.
4947 - Panneau pour cheminée (embroidery)
4948 - Dessus de cheminée (embroidery in collaboration with Dorothy Douglas-Binney)

1900 – (E.U.) 33 – L'attente (médaille de bronze)

1900 – (SAF) 219 - Portrait de Mlle E...

1901 – (SNBA) 145 - Danse espagnole.
146 - L'âge d'or.

5 rue Mixon, Paris (15th)

1902 – (SNBA) 184 - Bateaux en relâche à Cercy.

64 rue Notre-Dame-des-Champs, chez MM. Foinet et Lefebvre, Paris (6th)

1903 – (SNBA) 220 - Femme nue avec une rose.

13e expo. Société des Amis des arts de Nantes. 31 jan. - 15 mar. 1903.
5 rue Mizon, Paris (4th)

1903 – (NANTES) 44 - La jeune aveugle et l'Amour (400 fr)
45 - Têtes de Chérubins (400 fr)

3 rue Valentin-Haüy, Paris (15th)

1903 – (AUTOMNE) 100 - Une plume tombée de l'aile de l'Amour.
101- Portrait de Mme C...
102 - Portrait de Mme B...

1904 : Exposition Internationale de Nantes – Beaux-arts, 3 rue Valentin-Haüy, Paris (15th)

1904 – (NANTES) 79 - Sur le Canal de Bourgogne.
80 - Dolce far niente.

1904 – (SNBA) 209 - Après le bain.

Lille : Union artistique du Nord de la France. 3 rue Valentin Haüy, Paris.

1904 – (LILLE) 32 - Temps orageux (Etaples).
33 - Le Port à Circy-la-Tour.
34 - Ferme à Brignogan (Bretagne).

1904-Roubaix-Tourcoing : 26e Exposition Sté Artistique de Roubaix-Tourcoing. 18 Sept.- 29 Oct. 1904. Tableaux envoyés par le Ministère de l'Instruction Publique et des Beaux-Arts

1904 – (LILLE) 4 - Après le bain.

1905 – (SNBA) 223 - Endormies.
224 - Portrait de Mme B...
225 - Portrait de Mlle A. C...

24 boulevard des Invalides, Paris (7th)

1905 – (AUTOMNE) 267 - Portrait de Sir A. T.
268 - Portrait de Mlle N....
269 - Les Heures.
270 - Une Ville de province.

1906 – (SNBA) 195 - Vers Cythère.
196 - Une scène au bain.
197 - Portrait de Mme H. J... et ses filles.
198 - Saint-Paul à Londres (intérieur).

Lille : Union artistique du Nord de la France. 15 sept. – 1er nov. 1906. A Etaples

1906 – (LILLE) 33 - Endormies. Peinture à l'huile.
34 - La ronde. Peinture à l'huile.

Galerie Georges Petit. 24ème exposition de la Société internationale de Peinture & Sculpture. 7 – 31 décembre 1906. Peinture

1906 – 24 - Retour du jardin.
25 - Sieste.
26 - Rayon de soleil.
27 - Au soleil.
28 - Départ de bateaux.
29 - Après le départ.

Galerie Georges Petit. 25e exposition. Société internationale. 9 – 31 december 1907

1907 – 16 - Femme lisant.
17 - Le Volant déchiré.
18 - L'Attente (reproduced in original catalogue)

19 - La Lettre (reproduced in original catalogue)
20 - Pois de senteur.
21 - Pois de senteur.

3 rue Valentin Haüy (15th) et atelier 24 boulevard des Invalides, Paris (7th)

1907 – (SNBA) 202 - En été.
203 - Femme au miroir.
204 - A la fenêtre.
205 - Tête de femme.

1908 – (SNBA) 181 - Matinée d'été.
182 - Plage lointaine.

17e expo. Société des Amis des arts de Nantes. 31 jan. – 15 mar. 1908

1908 – (NANTES) 94 - Portrait de Mme B.
95 - La lettre (1000 fr)

Lille : Union artistique du Nord. 19 sept. – 1 nov. 1908. A Paris

1908 – (LILLE) 19 - Matine d'été (painting in oil)
20 - La lettre (painting in oil)

67 rue du Montparnasse, Paris (6th)

1909 – (SNBA) 183 - Le chant lointain.
184 - Nocturne.
185 - Au pied du mur.
186 - Le tour de cartes.
2309 - Panneau broderie.

1909 – (AUTOMNE) 230 - Mme Sada Yacco, 'Kesa'.
231 - Mme Sada Yacco, 'Kesa'.
232 - Mme Sada Yacco, 'Le Shogun' (scène de la folie).

Galerie Georges Petit. 27ème exposition de la Société internationale de Peinture & Sculpture. 7- 31 december 1909

1909 – 33 - Le Catalogue.
34 - Le Square Botton, à Rouen.
35 - Derniers beaux jours, Royan.
36 - Chercheurs d'huîtres.
37 - Promenade au bois.

1910 – (SNBA) 197 - Une nuit de canicule.
198 - Après la sieste.
199 - Conseil d'amie.
200 - La convalescence.

1910 – (AUTOMNE) 183 - Bacchannale.
184 - Vendange.

Amis des arts. 58e expo. Elève de M. J.-P. Laurens. Société nationale des Beaux-Arts

1910 – (BORDEAUX) 88 - En été (6000 fr)
89 - Retour du jardin (1500 fr)

Chez M. Lefebvre-Foinet, 19 rue Vavin (6th)

1911 – (SNBA) 214 - Au jardin du Luxembourg (Printemps 1900).
215 - Pêcheurs de crevettes (St-Georges).
216 - Le bel après-midi.
217 - Portrait de Mme L. B. et de ses enfants.

Amis des arts. 59e expo. Elève de MM. J.-P. Laurens et Léon Glaize

1911 – (BORDEAUX) 94 - Sainte Cécile.
95 - La tasse de chocolat.

19 rue Vavin, chez M. Lefebvre-Foinet, Paris (6th)

1912 – (SNBA) 226 - La sonate.
227 - L'Escarmouche.
228 - La coiffure.
229 - Au balcon.

Galerie Georges Petit. 30ème exposition de la Société internationale de Peinture & Sculpture. 6 -31 december 1912. 10 avenue Charles-Floquet, Paris (5th)

1912 – 19 - Maison à louer.
20 - L'Histoire du collier.
21 - Les Cerises.
22 - Au revoir.

10 avenue Charles-Floquet, Paris (5th)

1913 – (SNBA) 184 - Le bain de soleil.
185 - Silhouette estivale.

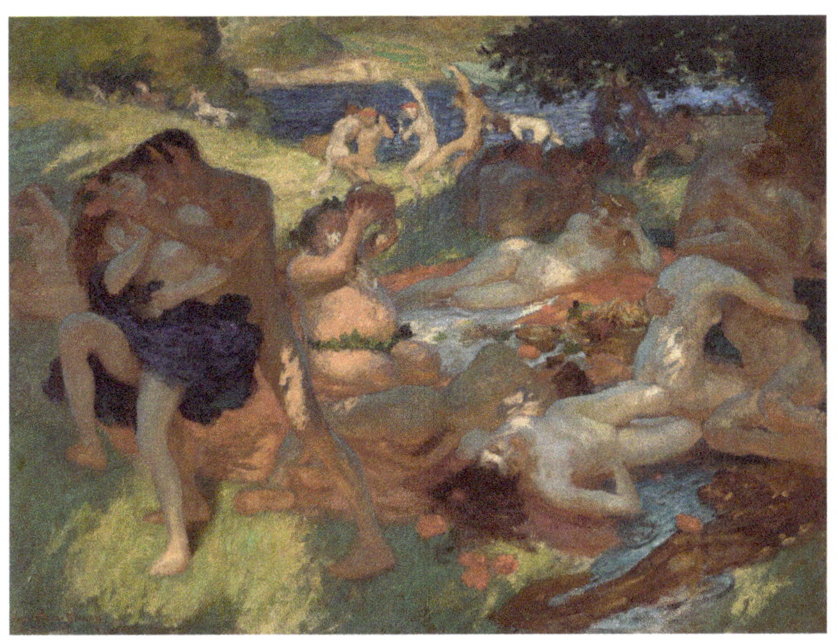

Bacchannalle - Shown at the Automne Salon 1910
oil on canvas on composition board, 113.0 x 149.5 cm
signed lower left: Rupert C W Bunny

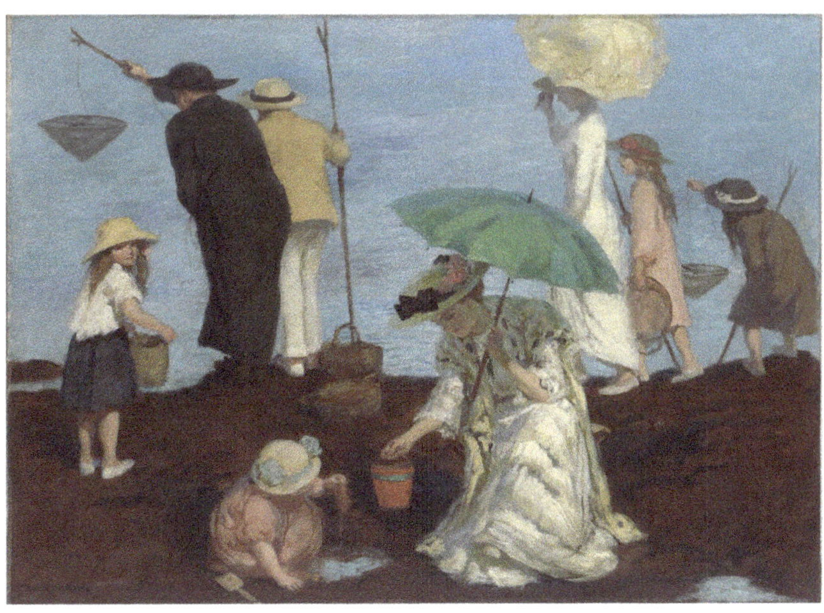

Pêcheurs de crevettes à Saint-Georges - Shown at SNBA 1911
oil on canvas, 120.7 x 161.9 cm
National Gallery of Victoria, Melbourne; Felton Bequest, 1946

186 - Portrait de Mlle D. J...

22e expo. Société des Amis des arts de Nantes. 7 feb. – 16 mar. 1913.

1913 – (NANTES) 48 - Au balcon (1300 fr)

1913 : 22e expo. Société des Amis des arts de Nantes. 7 feb. – 16 mar 1913. Supplément.

1913 – (NANTES) 499 - Jardin du Luxembourg. Printemps (4000 fr)

500 - Les cerises (1500 fr)

1913 – (AUTOMNE) 290 - Les Pléiades.

291 - Le Rite.

Galerie Georges Petit. 31ème exposition de la Société internationale de Peinture & Sculpture. 8 – 31 december 1913. Peinture. 10 avenue Charles-Floquet. Paris (5th)

1913 – 19 - Au bord de l'eau.

20 - A l'ombre.

21 - Fête de l'Assomption. Etaples.

22 - Consécration d'un calvaire. Etaples.

23 - La Quête. Etaples.

1914 – (SNBA) 184 - Centaures et océanides.

185 - Portrait du docteur K...

186 - Portrait de Mme B...

187 - Portrait de Mlle K...

Amis des arts. 62e expo. Elève de M. J.-P. Laurens. – Société nationale des Beaux-Arts : A. A Paris, 10 avenue Charles-Floquet, Paris (5th)

1914 – (BORDEAUX) 91 - Nuit d'été (3000 fr)

92 - La quête, Etaples (1000 fr)

Galerie Georges Petit. Grande Tombola des artistes et des écrivains français. 1 – 5 may 1915. Liste des lots (2ème liste)

1915 – Sur le balcon.

Galerie Georges Petit. 'La Guerre'. A partir du 12 may 1915. Tableaux & Aquarelles

1915 – 17 - Derniers arrivés attendant leur tour aux rayons X (ambulance américaine).

18 - Salle des bandages
(ambulance américaine).

Galerie Georges Petit. Exposition Rupert C. W. Bunny. 16-31 March 1917. Préface de Gustave Geffroy

1917 –

1 - Intérieur de Saint-Paul, à Londres, service de 4 heures ½ (November).
2 - Pêcheurs de crevettes, à Saint-Georges.
3 - Le Matin.
4 - Femme séchant ses cheveux.
5 - Le Bon Soleil.
6 - Le Petit Déjeuner.
7 - Les Marches ensoleillées.
8 - Le Lettre.
9 - Dévideuses.
10 - Causerie.
11 - Sous le palmier.
12 - Endormie.
13 - Chaude journée.
14 - Sous le prunier rouge.
15 - Dans l'allée.
16 - Au soleil.
17 - Matinée ensoleillée.
18 - Dolce farniente.
19 - Belle Matinée.
20 - Le Sécateur (femme cueillant des roses).
21 - La Terrasse.
22 - La Pompe.
23 - Le Journal.
24 - Femme mettant son écharpe.
25 - Femme lisant.
26 - La Dentelle accrochée.
27 - Reflet de miroir.
28 - Bain de soleil.

29 - Femme se séchant au soleil.
30 - Femme à la fenêtre.
31 - La Chaise longue.
32 - Premier essai.
33 - Ennui.
34 - La Chambre bleue.
35 - Le Peignoir vert.
36 - Rêverie.
37 - Chiffons.
38 - Le Tiroir.
39 - Femme au miroir.
40 - Les Ombres du rideau.
41 - Salle des bandages (ambulance américaine).
42 - La Cassette.
43 - Jeu de patience.
44 - Soleil d'hiver.
45 - Le Roman.
46 - Coiffure.
47 - Soir sur le balcon.
48 - Le Chant du rossignol.
49 - Les Cerises.
50 - Trèfle à quatre feuilles.
51 - Femme au chien.
52 - Tête de femme russe.
53 - La Matinée japonaise.

Galerie Georges Petit. Exposition au profit de la Fraternité des Artistes. 13 – 29 April 1917. Tableaux

1917 – 8 - Jeu de patience.

Galerie Georges Petit. 32ème exposition de la Société internationale de Peinture & Sculpture. 12 December 1917 – 10 January 1918. Paintings. 18 rue Pierre-Nicole, Paris (5th)

1917 – 20 - Après la baignade.
21 - La Chambre bleue.
22 - Femme à la glace.

23 - Jeu de patience.
24 - Causerie.

Galerie Georges Petit. 2ème Exposition au profit de la Fraternité des Artistes. 6 –28 April 1918. Tableaux.

1918 – 8 - En promenade.

18 rue Pierre-Nicole, Paris (5th)

1919 – (SNBA) 1704 - Daphné et Apollon.
1705 - Hephaestos et ses servantes en or.
1706 - Nausicaa et ses suivantes.

1919 – (AUTOMNE) 272 - Salomé.
273 - Circé.
274 - La Toison d'or.

1920 – (SNBA) 274 - Courtisanes à la campagne.
275 - Echo et Narcisse.

Élève de J.-P. Laurens, 18 rue Pierre Nicole, Paris (5th)

1920 – (LYON) (SNBA) 163 - Femme à la fenêtre..

1920 – (AUTOMNE) 338 - Les Danaïdes.
339 - Danse d'amour.
340 - Vénus et Adonis.

Amis des arts. 64e expo. Elève de Jean-Paul Laurens. Société nationale des Beaux-Arts

1920 – (BORDEAUX) 79 - Femme à l'écharpe (1500 fr)
80 - Femme lisant (1500 fr)

1921 – (SNBA) 209 - L'Abri.
210 - Sur un balcon (Champs de Mars).
211 - Une salle d'ambulance américaine.
212 - La Sonate.

1921 – (AUTOMNE) 309 - L'eau du Styx.
310 - Oedipe et le Sphinx.

Galerie Georges Petit. Exposition Rupert Bunny. Monotypes. 16 – 31 March 1921

1921 – 1 - Capture.
2 - La Danse.
3 - Danse de bergers.
4 - Le Retour de Perséphone.
5 - Ménades.

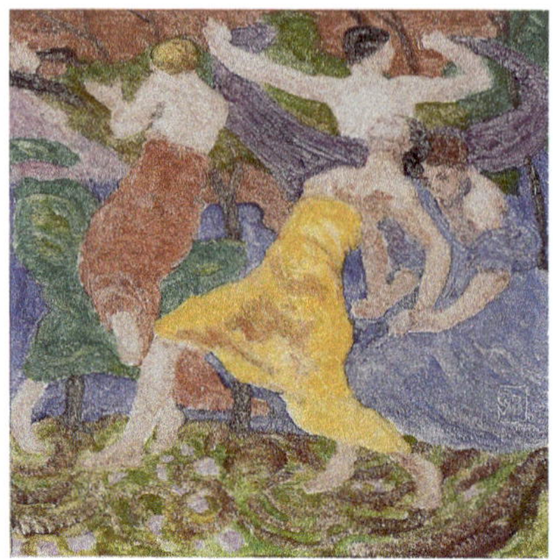

Rupert Bunny:
Fresque, 1921. AGNSW.

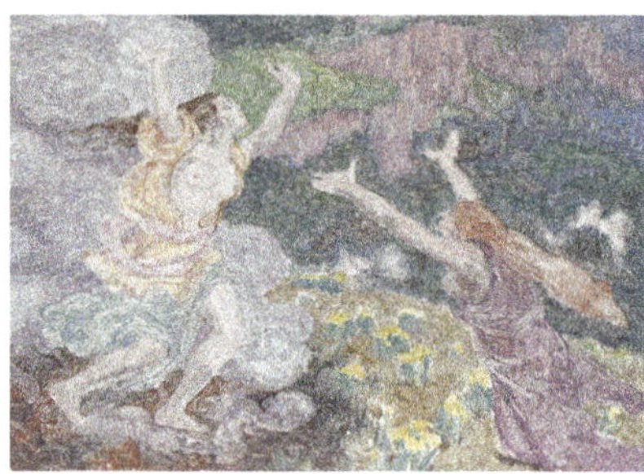

Rupert Bunny:
Le Retour de Perséphone, 1921.

6 - Femme orientale.
7 - Danse.
8 - Danse au harem.
9 - La Toilette de la favorite.
10 - Fresque.
11 - Idylle.
12 - Femme couchée.
13 - Anges.
14 - Après le bain.
15 - Atalante.
16 - Les Nymphes des rochers bleus.
17 - Terpsichore.
18 - Baigneuses.
19 - Suzanne.
20 - Le Tub.
21 - Danse.
22 - Arabesque.
23 - Aurore et Séléné.
24 - La Danse du voile.
25 - Le Bain au désert.
26 - Les Fruits.
27 - Rêverie.
28 - La Femme de Putiphar.
29 - Jeune Fille en bleu.
30 - La Toilette.
31 - Zéphyr enlevant Psyché.
32 - Danse du printemps.
33 - L'Offrande.
34 - La Circassienne.
35 - La Couvée.
36 - La Coiffure.
37 - Femme au cygne.
38 - Fantaisie.
39 - Au harem.
40 - Danse de bacchantes.

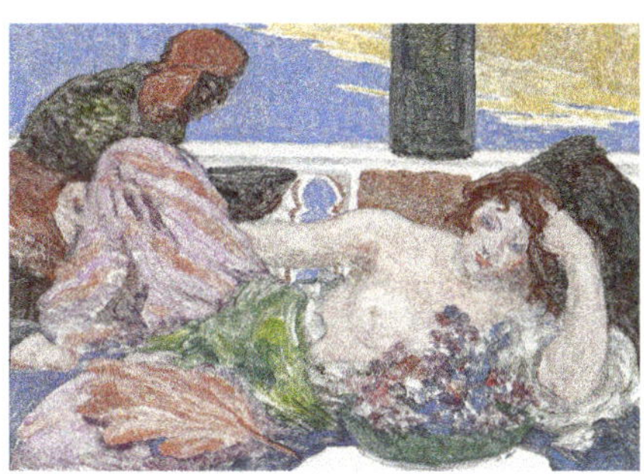

Rupert Bunny: *Odalisque,* 1921.

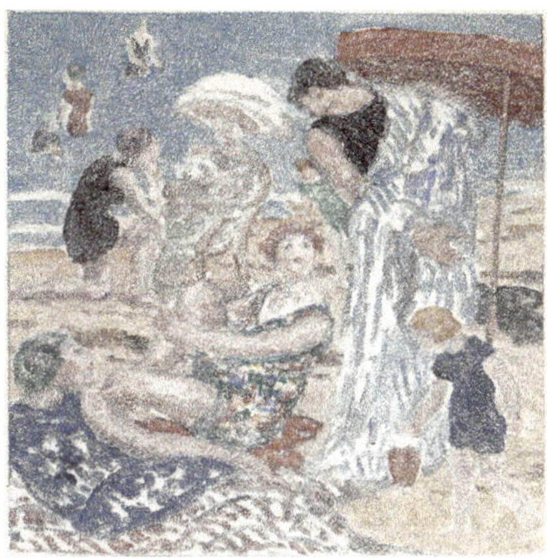

Rupert Bunny: *Sur La Plage,* 1921.

41 - Odalisque.
42 - Concours.
43 - L'Oracle.
44 - Le Bain de soleil.
45 - Le Bain de soleil.
46 - Danse rituelle.
47 - La Coiffeuse.
48 - La Cassette.
49 - Le Nid.
50 - La Lecture.
51 - Fresque.
52 - Bacchantes.
53 - Aux Nymphes.
54 - Danse au harem.
55 - La Tireuse de cartes.
56 - La Fontaine de Vénus.
57 - Danse.
58 - Phoebus et Artémise.
59 - La Fenêtre fleurie.
60 - Bacchanale.
61 - La Route.
62 - Circé et Picumnus.
63 - La Favorite.
64 - L'Esclave.
65 - Sur la plage.

1922 – (SNBA) 143 - Femme au chapeau brun.

1922 – (AUTOMNE) 335 - Hylas.
336 - Héraklès au Jardin des Hespérides.

Galerie Georges Petit. Exposition Rupert Bunny. May 1922

1922 – (the catalogue for this exhibition has not been found)

Galerie Devambez. Quelques études de la Femme. 24 April to 10 May 1922

1922 – 9 - Europa.
10 - Femme russe.

1923 – (SNBA) 156 - L'Hymne du Matin.

157 - Héraklès et les nymphes de l'Himora.
158 - Automne (pour un dessus de cheminée).
159 - Europa

1923 – (AUTOMNE) 247 - La Grotte de Styx.

Galerie Devambez. Exposition de Paravents, panneaux décoratifs, écrans. From 24 October to 10 November 1923

1923 – (the description of the works in this exhibition is not available).

1924 – (SNBA) 154 - Sur le tapis de varech.
155 - Trois pauvres.

1924 – (AUTOMNE) 265 - La fille de Jephté.
266 - Ménades.

Galerie Georges Petit. Exposition de Monotypes par Rupert Bunny. Open from 16 to 30 October 1924

1924 –
1 - Capture.
2 - La Danse.
3 - Danse de Bergers.
4 - Le Retour de Perséphone.
5 - Ménades.
6 - Femme orientale.
7 - Danse.
8 - Danse au harem.
9 - Fresque.
10 - Idylle.
11 - Femme couchée.
12 - Anges.
13 - Après le bain.
14 - Atalante.
15 - Les Nymphes des rochers bleus.
16 - Terpsichore.
17 - Baigneuses.
18 - Suzanne.
19 - Le Tub.

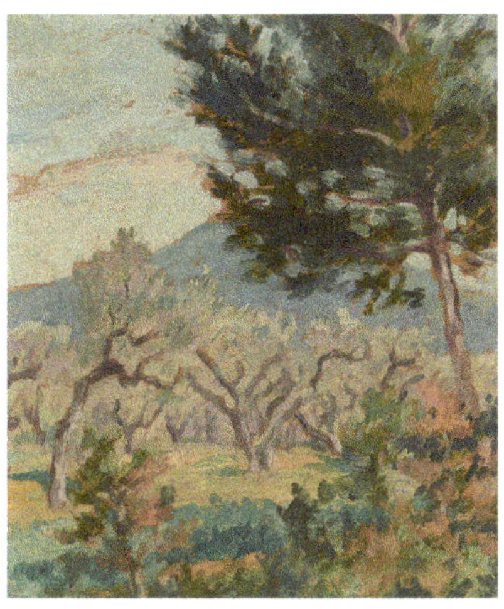

Rupert Bunny:
Olive Tree, Afternoon, La Lavandou.
1924.

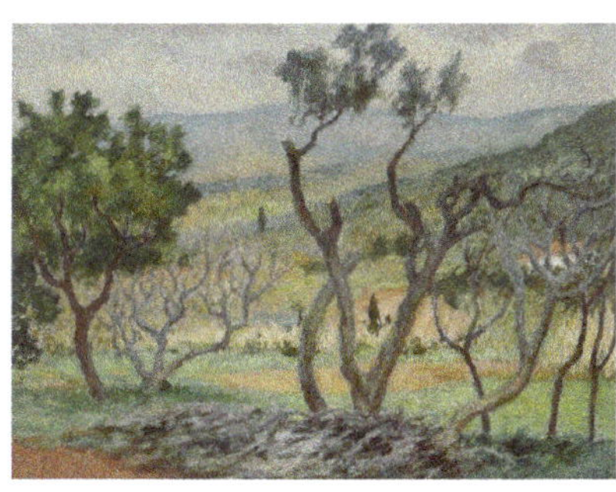

Rupert Bunny:
Landscape, South of France, 1924.

20 - Danse.
21 - Arabesque.
22 - Le Bain au désert.
23 - Les Fruits.
24 - La Femme de Putiphar.
25 - La Toilette.
26 - Zéphire enlevant Psyché.
27 - Danse du Printemps.
28 - La Circassienne.
29 - La Coiffure.
30 - Fantaisie.
31 - Au Harem.
32 - Odalisque.
33 - L'Oracle.
34 - Le Bain de soleil.
35 - Danse rituelle.
36 - La Cassette.
37 - Fresque.
38 - Bacchantes.
39 - Aux Nymphes.
40 - Danse au harem.
41 - La Fontaine de Vénus.
42 - Phœbus et Artémise.
43 - La Fenêtre fleurie.
44 - Bacchanale.
45 - Sur la plage.
46 - Circé.
47 - Les Cymbales.
48 - Le Paradis de Mahomet.
49 - Les Héliades.
50 - L'Offrande.
51 - Porteuse d'eau.
52 - Nymphes au bord de la mer.
53 - Le Sommeil d'Endymion.
54 - Hylas.

55 - Le Châtiment.
56 - Femme se coiffant.
57 - La Fontaine des Nymphes.
58 - Danse au harem.
59 - Paysans antiques.
60 - Les Figues de Barbarie.
61 - Le Jardin des Nymphes.
62 - Le Rite.
63 - Trois Femmes dans un paysage.

1925 – (SNBA) 62 - Temps de sècheresse.
685 - Le chantier du bâtiment des P. T. R.
686 - Boulevard Montparnasse.

1925 – (AUTOMNE) 188 - Garçon et jeune fille.
189 - Nymphes prophétiques.

36 rue Pierre-Nicole, Paris (5th)

1926 – (SNBA) 144 - Des femmes esclaves.
145 - Nausicaa.

1927 – (AUTOMNE) 305 – 'L'offrande'.
306 - Peleus et Thétis.

1929 – (SNBA) 235 - La mort de Laodamia.
236 - Compagnes de Nausicaa.

Galerie Georges Petit. Exposition Rupert Bunny. Paysages du Midi. 16 – 30 November 1929

1929 – 1 - Paysage : Bandol.
2 - La Bastide : le Lavandou.
3 - Cabane rouge : le Lavandou.
4 - Maisons de vignerons : Port-Vendres.
5 - Un Clos à Bandol.
6 - Près de Bandol.
7 - La Gare de Bandol.
8 - Villas près Bandol.
9 - Le Poirier.
10 - Bandol.
11 - Pâté de maisons (Var).

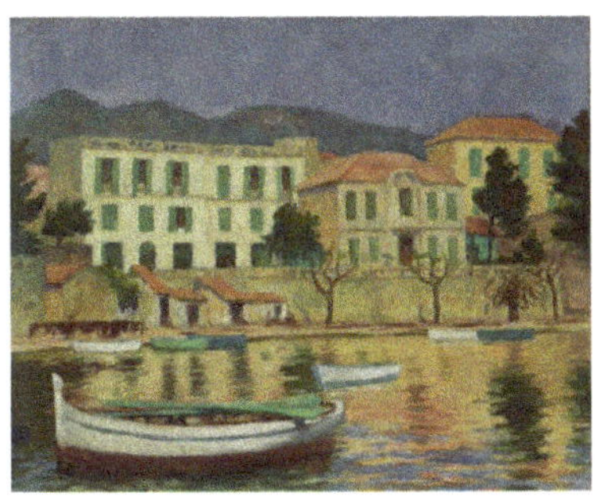

Rupert Bunny: *Bandol,* 1929.

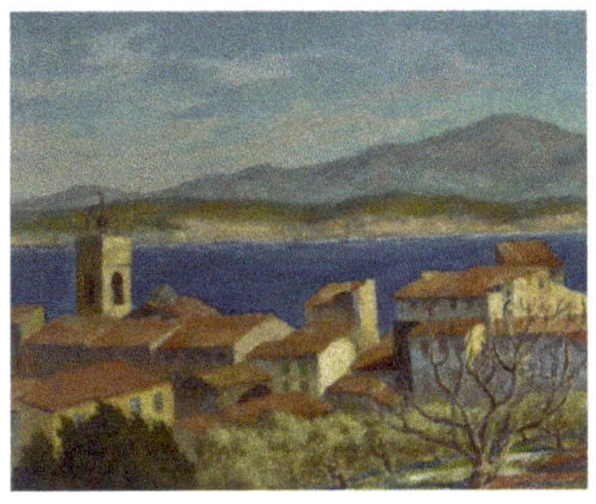

Rupert Bunny:
Blue Day, Bandol. 1929.

12 - Orage (Var).
13 - Maisonnettes : Bandol.
14 - Maison rose : Bandol.
15 - Ferme près de Bandol.
16 - Falaise : Bandol.
17 - Bandol : jour de mistral.
18 - Bandol : jour gris.
19 - Falaises à Avignon.
20 - La Porte rose.
21 - Rochers près Sanary.
22 - Coteau du Var.
23 - Colline près Bandol.
24 - Bandol, vue du môle.
25 - Village abandonné (Var).
26 - Près Bandol.
27 - Arbres gelés, Bandol.
28 - Le Château des Papes.
29 - Le Quai : Bandol.
30 - Hôtel Beau-Rivage.
31 - Bateaux blancs : Bandol.
32 - Maison rouge : le Lavandou.
33 - Le Port : Bandol.
34 - La Côte : Six-Fours.
35 - Village de Six-Fours.
36 - Villas à Sanary.
37 - Fleurs.
38 - Paysages d'Australie.
39 - Le Creek de Cudgewa.
40 - Les Alpes Australiennes.
41 - Dans les Upper-Murray.

1930 – (SNBA)

319 - Saltimbanques.
320 - La Fontaine.
321 - Danse.
322 - Fleurs.
323 - Fleurs.

1931 – (SNBA) 314 - Danse antique.
315 - Paysans devant leur maison.
316 - Fontaine sacrée.
317 - Fleurs.
318 - Fleurs.

1931 – (AUTOMNE) 268 - L'Aube.
269 - Marée basse.

1932 – (SNBA) 279 - Silhouettes.
280 - Jeunes filles en vacances.

BURGE Maud
Born May 1865 Wellington, NZ, died 1957.
37 Fleet Street, chez Mrs. Hoare, London, G.B.

1922 – (SAF) 297 - Dans le jardin, château de Deux-Rives.

BURGESS Arthur James Wetherall
Born 1879 Bombala, Australia. died 1957 London.
Elève de M. Julius Olsson. 6, Saint-John's Wood Studios, London, G.B.

1908 – (SAF) 281 - Désespéré.
2 Marlborough Studios, Finchley Road 12A, London G.B.

1912 – (SAF) 300 – 'Le ressac', près Scarborough.
8 Stanley Gardens, Belsize Park, London, G.B.

1914 – (SAF) 336 - Le sillage.

BURNETT-NATHAN Adélaïde A. or **NATHAN** Mlle Adelaïde-Burnett : **BURNETT** or **BRUNETT**
Born Sydney
Elève de MM. A. Ludovici et H. Gervex. Chez M. Disand, 54 rue du Faubourg-Poissonnière, Paris (9th)

1887 – (SAF) 3295 - Portrait de Mlle Marie Gourieff ((pastel)).
Elève de MM. H. Gervex et Ludovici. Chez Mme Disand, 54 rue du Faubourg-Poissonnière (9th)

1888 – (SAF) 2759 - Olga (design).

1889 – (SAF) 2930 - Une petite Luxembourgeoise : portrait de Léonie G… (design).

BUTLER Margaret

Born 30 April 1883 Greymouth, Wellington, New Zealand, died 4 September 1947 Wellington, NZ.

Elève de Antoine Boudelle, 18 rue Antoine Bourdelle, Paris (15th)

1927– (TUILERIES)	2643 - Buste de Bretonne.	

Hôtel Lutétia, boulevard Raspail, Paris (14th)

1928– (TUILERIES	436 - Tête d'enfant (bronze)	
	437 - Vieil homme (wood)	
1929– (TUILERIES)	206 - Tête de femme.	

17 rue Campagne-Première (14th)

1930– (TUILERIES)	468 - Rosalie, tête (bronze)	
	469 - Berto, tête (bronze)	

Ester Hazy Gasse, 30 Vienne (6th)

1932– (TUILERIES)	270 - Tête de jeune homme.	

Hôtel Lutétia, Boulevard Raspail (14th)

1933– (TUILERIES)	380 - Sculpture.	
	381 - Sculpture.	

[supplément] : 4 rue de Chevreuse (6th)

1933– (TUILERIES)	2680	Esther (plaster bust)

Galerie Hébrard, 8 rue Royale (8th)

1934– (TUILERIES)	354 (s)	Jeune fille (projet pour fontaine).

114 The Terrace Wellington, New Zealand

1938– (TUILERIES)	284 (p)	La Nouvelle Zélande.
	285 (p)	Une petite fleur sauvage.

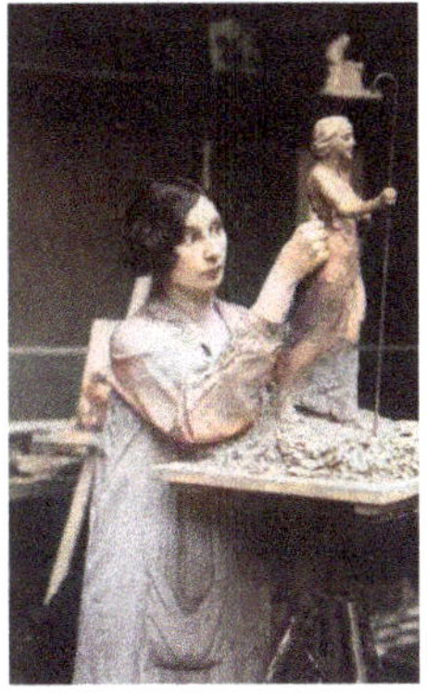

Margaret Butler in her Paris Studio, 1930.

C

CARRICK-FOX Ethel, or **CARRICK,** Ethel

Born 7 February 1872 Uxbridge, London G.B., died 17 June 1952 Melbourne

65 boulevard Arago, Paris (13th)

1906 – (AUTOMNE) 296 - Portrait de Mlle M...
297 - Etude.

1906 – (SNBA) 232 - Le Printemps.

1907 – (SNBA) 245 - Le marché.

65 boulevard Arago (13th) et chez M. Paul Foinet fils, 21 rue Bréa, Paris (6th)

1907 – (AUTOMNE) 272 - Jeune femme riant.
273 - Marché aux fleurs à Venise.
274 - Marché aux fleurs.
275 - Marché aux faïences.
275 bis - A Venise.
276 - Les enfants s'amusent.

1908 – (SNBA) 212 - Au Luxembourg.
213 - Au Luxembourg.

65 boulevard Arago, Paris (13th)

1908 – (AUTOMNE) 359 - La Promenade.
360 - Au Marché (sketch).
361 - Esquisse en Australie.
362 - Esquisse en Australie.

1909 – (AUTOMNE) 257 - Nature morte.
258 - Au Luxembourg : Le Diabolo.
259 - Au Luxembourg : Au mois de mars.
260 - En Australie.

16ème Exposition de la Libre Esthétique – 7 Mars – 12 Avril 1909.

65 boulevard Arago, Paris (13th)

1909 – (LIBRE ESTHETIQUE)
37 - Portrait de Mlle M.

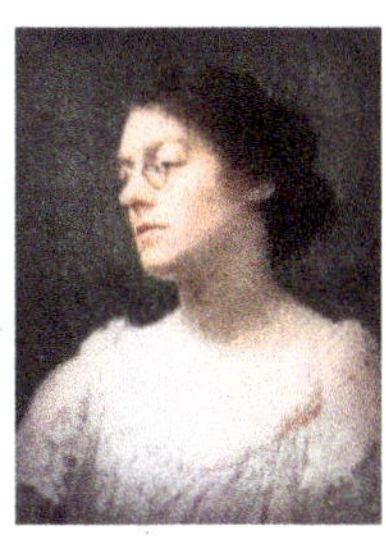

	38 - Portrait de jeune femme.
	39 - La Promenade.
	40 - Nourrices et bébés.
	41 - Le Diabolo.
	42 - La Petite Rose.
	43 - Le Marché.
	44 - Un Marché aux fleurs à Venise.
1910 – (SNBA)	229 - Marché aux fleurs.
1910 – (AUTOMNE)	200 - Au Luxembourg.
	201 - Effet blanc.
	202 - Sur la plage.
1911 – (SNBA)	246 - Effet de contre-jour.
	247 - Sur la plage.
1911 – (AUTOMNE)	250 - Laveuses Algériennes.
	251 - Un Papillon.
	252 - Femme Arabe.
	253 - Vue de Cadix.
1912 – (SNBA)	268 - La marée haute à St-Malo.
	269 - Le port d'Alger.
1912 – (AUTOMNE)	295 - Jeune homme contre une fenêtre.
	296 - Portrait de M. Penleigh Boyd.
	297 - Deux dames et un jeune poète.
	298 - Sur le quai à Dinard.
	299 - Marché à Bou-Saada.
	300 - Marché algérien.

65 boulevard Arago, Paris (13th)

1913 – (SOCIETE DES PEINTRES ORIENTALISTES)

	47 - Le port d'Alger.
	148 - La mosquée de Tanger.
	149 - Une rue à Tanger.
	150 - Le marché de Bou-Saâda.
	151 - Le marché aux chameaux.
1919 – (AUTOMNE)	315 - Mme de Marquette.
	316 - Mary (peint pendant le bombardement de Paris 1918).
	317 - Coin du marché à Tahiti.

318 - Sur une plage australienne.

1920 – (SNBA) 299 - Les baigneuses.
300 - Jour de l'an en Australie.
301 - Journée chaude (Australie).

1920 – (AUTOMNE) 393 - L'Attente.
394 - Le Sourire.
395 - Coin de mon jardin.

1921 – (SNBA) 244 - Une Bretonne (Portrait).
245 - Journée de septembre (plein-air).

1921 – (SDAI) 550 - Soucis.
551 - Fleurs d'automne.
552 - Dans le jardin du Luxembourg.
553 - Monotype.
554 - Monotype.

1921 – (AUTOMNE) 366 - L'Alsacienne.
367 - Mme Alfred Thiroux.
368 - La rue Saussier à Kairouan.

1922 – (SNBA) 170 - Au dessert.

1922 – (AUTOMNE) 411 - Jeune femme à la rose

1923 – (SNBA) 190 - Nature morte.
191 - Portrait d'une sœur belge.

1923 – (AUTOMNE) 284 - Portrait de M. Oliver Madox Hueffer.
285 - Portrait de M. Jean Batalla.

1924 – (SNBA) 179 - Marie dans son jardin.
180 - Soleil d'été.

1924 – (AUTOMNE) 314 - Le marché à Vérone.
314 bis - Le Vieux Pont à Florence.

1926 – (AUTOMNE) 544 - Pivoines.
545 - Place Saint-Médard, Paris.
546 - Rue à Kairouan.
547 - Esquisse.
548 - Esquisse.

1927 – (SNBA) 224 - Marché aux légumes (Nice).
225 - Marché aux fleurs (Nice).
226 - Marché aux poissons (Nice).

1927 – (AUTOMNE)	344 - Marché aux fleurs, Nice.
	345 - Cagnes.
1928 – (SNBA)	339 - Le printemps dans le Tyrol.
	340 - Marché aux fleurs à Nice.
1928 – (AUTOMNE)	323 - Monte-Carlo.
	324 - Anémones.
1929 – (SNBA)	287 - Intérieur.
	288 - Place St-Médard, Paris.
	289 - Souvenir.
1929 – (AUTOMNE)	236 - Le Pont Napoléon, Paris.
	237 - Chanson d'un oiseau.
1930 – (SNBA)	371 - Tulipes.
1930 – (AUTOMNE)	416 - Le Pont-Neufr
	417 - Le Quai des Orfèvres.
	418 - Printemps sur le Quai des Grands-Augustins.
	419 - L'après-midi sur le Quai des Grands-Augustins.
1931 – (SNBA)	379 - Les femmes, l'amour et les fleurs.
1931 – (AUTOMNE)	314 - Fleurs du jardin.
	315 - Fleurs sauvages.
1932 – (SNBA)	346 - Pivoines.
	347 - Marché aux fleurs, Nice.
	348 - Marché aux fleurs, Nice.
1932 – (AUTOMNE)	257 - Tulipes.
	258 - Anémones.
1933 – (SNBA)	378 - L'Eté.
	379 - Le petit déjeuner.
	380 - Tulipes.
1934 – (AUTOMNE)	302 bis - Le jour de la lessive.
	302 ter - Dans la cuisine.
	302 quarter - Une apparition dans les vignes.
	302 quint - Fleurs d'automne.
1935 – (SNBA)	293 - Le corsage rose.

1935 – (TUILERIES) 343 - M. Louis Ridel.
344 - Une rue à Nice.
345 - Fleurs de printemps.

1937 – (SAF) 260 - Le bac, Kashmir.

1937 – (AUTOMNE) 270 - Femmes musulmanes dans un jardin.
271 - Portrait.

1938 – (AUTOMNE) 287 - Le marché, Darjeeling.
288 - Le printemps dans le Tyrol.

1939 – (SNBA) 202 - Marché aux fleurs.
203 - Marché aux fleurs.

CHAPMAN Clara Véra, a.k.a. Mrs Vera Eichelbaum
Born Dunedin, New Zealand 1885, died 1953

6 rue Boissonade, Paris (14th)

1911 – (INDEPENDANTS) 1278 - Portrait d'une dame.
1279 - Caveau des Innocents.
1280 - Paysage.
1281 - Rue à Paris.

CHAPMAN Grace Evelyn
Born October 25 1888, Marrickville NSW, died London, UK 1961

Villa Elisa, 6, Rue Jean-Daval, Dieppe, France.

1920 – (SNBA) 1092 - Ruines de l'église de *Villers-Bretonneux.*
1093 - Vieilles maisons ensoleillées.
1094 - Une vieille cour à Saint-Ines (Angleterre).

Hôtel Select, à Dieppe, France.

1921 – (SNBA) 1237 - Godshuis. Bruges (Aquarelle).
1238 - Le quai vert (coucher de soleil) (aquarelle).
1239 - L'entrée du Béguinage. Bruges (aquarelle).

Grand Hôtel du Commerce, 39, rue St-Jacques, à Bruges, Belgium.

1922 – (SNBA) 1033 - L'entrée du Béguinage, Bruges l'après-midi (aquarelle).

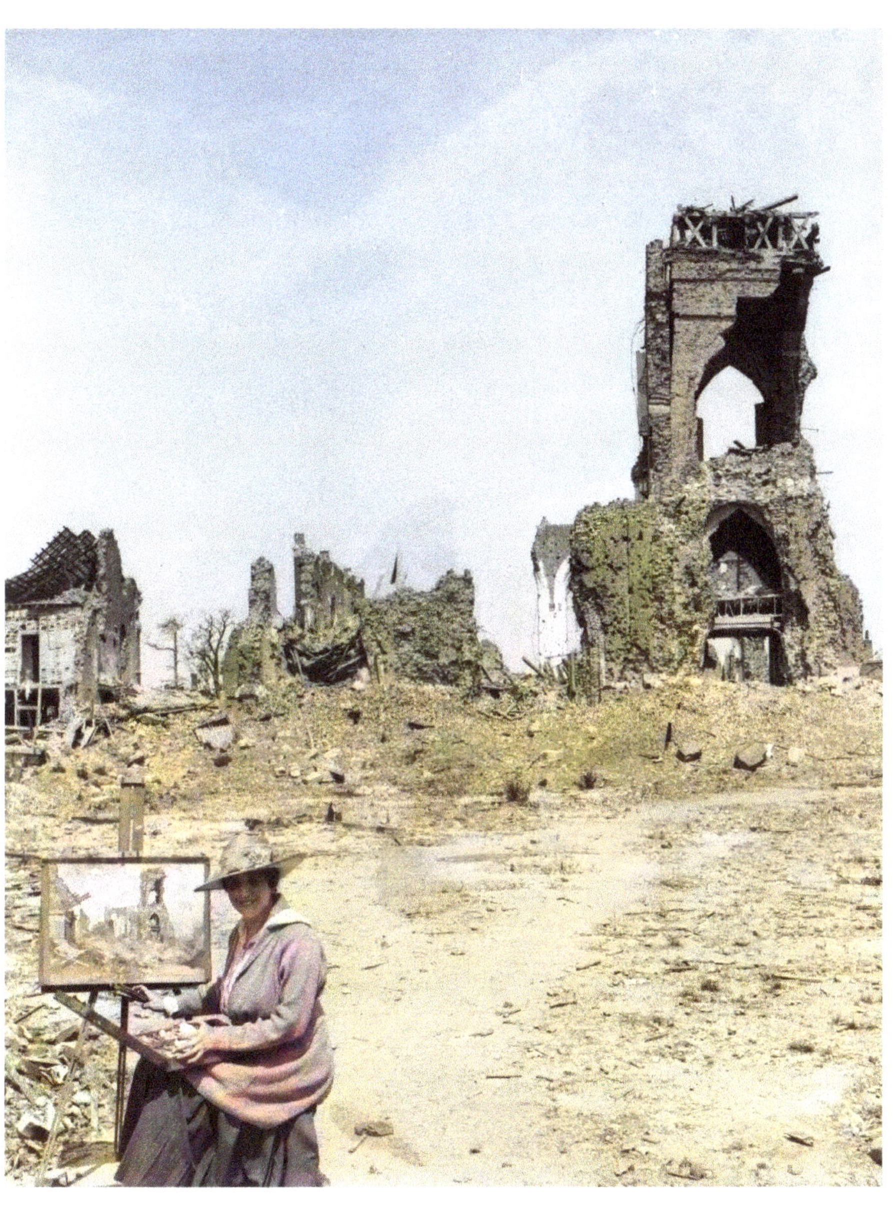

Evelyn Chapman at Villers Bretonneaux 1919.

1034 - Pont du Cheval, Bruges (aquarelle).
1035 - L'après-midi au Béguinage, Bruges (aquarelle).

Hôtel Select, Dieppe, France.

1923 – (SNBA) 1464 - Un Canal. Venise (aquarelle).

CHAPMAN William Ernest

Born 1847 Wellington, New Zealand, died 1945 Melbourne, Victoria.

5 rue Monsieur, Paris (7th)

1893 – (SAF) 372 - Les sœurs.

65 boulevard Arago, Paris (13th)

1894 – (SNBA) 231 - Pastorale.
232 - Caroline.

COATES George James

1869 Melbourne, Australia, died 1930 London, G.B.

Elève de MM. Jean-Paul Laurens et Benjamin Constant. 63 avenue du Maine, Paris (14th)

1898 – (SAF) 493 - Portrait de M. D...

1899 – (SAF) 475 - Portrait.

1900 – (SAF) 310 - Portrait de Mme D...

Elève de Benjamin Constant et de M. J.-P. Laurens. 12 Spring Bridge, Ealing, London G.B.

1904 – (SAF) 439 - Portrait de ma femme.

Elève de M. Benjamin-Constant et de M. Jean-Paul Laurens. 9 Trafalgar Studios, Chelsea, G.B..

1907 – (SAF) 1853 - Portrait de Mme C… (design)

1908 – (SAF) 406 – 'Ritenuto'.

1909 – (SAF) 430 - Portrait de Mme la baronne de S...

Elève de Benjamin Constant et de M. Jean-Paul Laurens, 1 Cedar Studios, Glebe Place, Chelsea, G.B.

1910 – (SAF) 484 - Portrait of Miss Jessica Strubell.

1911 – (SAF) 430 - Portrait d'une dame américaine.
431 - Portrait de Miss Inez Hicks.

1912 – (SAF) 429 - Portrait de Mme Bennett.
430 – 'Théâtreuse'.

55 Glebe Place, Chelsea, London G.B.

1914 – (SNBA) 256 - Mrs. Griffits and Nancy.
1919 – (SNBA) 1740 - Portrait du Colonel Sir Bruce-Porter, Knight Commander of the British Empire, companion of the Order of St-Michael and St-George (military division), army medical service.
1923 – (SNBA) 225 - Prête à danser.
1924 – (SNBA) 223 - Portrait de Mrs Henry Daman.
1925 – (SNBA) 95 - Un vieillard de la guerre civile américaine.

COFFEY Alfred R.
Born 1869 Limerick, Ireland; died 1950 Sydney
17 Nassau Street, chez Bourlet and Sons Ltd., London, G.B.
1935 – (SAF) 546 - The portal of a great city.

COHEN Isaac Michael
Born 1884 Ballarat, Australia; died 1951 London
42ª Linden Gardens, London, G.B.
1925 – (SAF) 173 - Winifred, fille de M. le major et *Madame J.-B. Paget.*

COLAHAN Colin
Born 1897 Woodend, Victoria, Australia, died 1987 Ciotti, Italy
12 boulevard de Clichy, Paris (9th)
1923 – (AUTOMNE) 388 - Le Pont Saint-Michel: crépuscule (1000 fr)
1924 – (SAF) 479 - La robe chinoise (portrait de moi-même).
480 - Portrait.
5 rue Barrault, Paris (13th)
1925 – (SAF) 257 - Portrait de moi-même.
1926 – (SAF) 477 - Portrait de moi-même.
5 Hillsleigh Road, London G.B.
1938 – (TUILERIES) 356 - Le Volet bleu.
1939 – (TUILERIES) 323 - Sous-bois à Saint-Cloud.
324 - Le canal de Chartres.

325 - Portrait de l'artiste.

COLQUHOUN Archibald Douglas

Born 26 October 1894 Melbourne, Australia, died 14 May 1983 Melbourne, Victoria.

147 rue Broca, Paris (13th)

1925 – (AUTOMNE) 287 – 'La Vieille Tour'.

1925 – (SAF) 263 - Portrait de jeune fille.

(SAF) 180 - Etude de fleurs.

1926 – (SAF) 491 - Nature morte.

CONDER Charles Edward

Born 24 October 1868 Middlesex, G.B., died 9 February 1909 Virginia Water, Surrey, G.B.

13 rue de Ravignan, Paris (18th)

1892 – (SNBA) 255 - Les Roses.

256 - La Perle.

Les Champs d'or.

14 rue de Navarin, Paris (9th)

1893 – (SNBA) 241 - Juillet (Vétheuil).

242 - Soir d'été.

243 – 'Mayday'.

244 - Juin (Chantemesle).

5e Exposition des Peintres Impressionnistes et Symbolistes (Galerie Le Barc de Boutteville, Paris, October - November 1893)

1893 - 38 - Les baigneurs (fan).

39 - Les baigneurs (fan).

6e Exposition des Peintres Impressionnistes et Symbolistes (Galerie Le Barc de Boutteville, Paris, March 1894)

1894 35 - Fan.

36 - Fan

7e Exposition des Peintres Impressionnistes et Symbolistes (Galerie Le Barc de Boutteville, Paris, July 1894)

1894 - 40 - Fleuve (aquarelle).

41 - Intérieur XVIIIe siècle (aquarelle).

13 rue de Ravignan, Paris (18th).

1894 – (SNBA) 270 - Marine - mer grise et nuages.

271 - Marine - mer bleue et falaises.
272 - Marine - mer verte et ombre.
273 - Paysage avec personnage.
274 - Paysage.
275 - Paysage : une moisson.

A l'Art Nouveau (S. Bing), 22 rue de Provence, Paris (8th)

1896 – (SNBA) 216 – Trois panneaux peints sur pour la decoration d'un boudoir

Chez M. Hacon, 38 rue Aguado, Dieppe, France

1898 – (SNBA) 1414 – Souvenir sentimental
1415 – Soir d'été.
1416 – Fantasie byzantine.
1417 - Eventail bleu
1418 - Eventail beige
1419 - '1826'

1898 – *International Society of Sculptors, Painters, Gravers, London*
91 – Blossom
226 – Design for a Fan.
235 - Landscape

14 Wellington Square, London, G.B.

1904 – (SNBA) 287 - La fontaine.
288 - La promenade.
289 - Au grand Canal (Venise).
290 - Les meules

1913 – Armory Show, Chicago
68 – The Beautiful Antonia, 1902
69 – Fantasia, silk panel
70 – Casino de Paris (on silk)
71 – The Toilet.
72 – The Crinolines.
73 – Etching.
74 – Lithograph in red.

1913 - Armory Show, Boston
27 – The Beautiful Antonia, 1902
28 – Fantasia, silk panel

29 – Casino de Paris (on silk)
30 – The Toilet, pastel.
31 - The Crinolines.

1913 – Armory Show, New York

569 – The Beautiful Antonia, 1902.
570 - Fantasia, silk panel
571- Casino de Paris (on silk)
572 - The Toilet, pastel.
573 – The Guitar Player, sanguine, 1904.
1020 - The Crinolines.
1074 – Litho in red.
1075 – Etching.

CORDOVA Jose
Born Melbourne, Australia

1 rue Juliette-Lamber, Paris (17th)

1890 – (SAF) 603 - Portrait de Mlle L. D...

CRANE Olive Catherine
Born 1895 Sydney, Australia, died 1935 Sydney

1924 – (SAF) 4387 - Illustrations de *Bab Ballado* (etching)
4388 - Illustrations de *Bab Ballado* (etching)

1925 – (SAF) 2171 - Illustration de *Louise* (etching)

CROWLEY Grace Adela Williams
Born 28 May 1890 Barraba, NSW, Australia, died 21 April 1979 Manly, NSW.

16 bis, rue Bardinet, Atelier 25, Paris (14th)

1928 – (AUTOMNE) 458 - Portrait.

CARTER Norman St Clair
Born 30 June 1875 Kew, Victoria Australia, died 18 September 1963, Gordon, New South Wales.

1913 – 348 - Portrait de Mlle X...
aka A Low Toned Harmony
(médaille de 3ème classe)

D

DANCIGER Alice

Born 1914 Antwerp, Belgium, died 21 April 1991 Sydney, NSW.

40 rue Boissonade, Paris (14th)

1936– (TUILERIES) 395 - Portrait.

DAVIDSON Bessie Ellen

Born 22 May 1879 Adelaide, Australia, died 22 February 1965 Montparnasse, France.

Elève de MM. Raphaël Collin, G. Courtois et R. Miller ; 7 rue Léopold-Robert, Paris (14th)

1905 – (SAF) 528 - Grand'mère bretonne.
529 - La petite Marie.

2 rue Bréa, chez M. Lefebvre-Foinet, Paris (6th)

1906 – (SNBA) 358 - Le Luxembourg.
359 - Dans la rue.

64 rue Madame, Paris (6th)

1911 – (SNBA) 371 - Dame en robe blanche.
372 - Dame en robe bleue.

1912 – (SNBA) 384 - Portrait de Mlle G. D...
385 - Le livre vert. Le boîte de bijoux (intérieur).

18 rue Boissonade, Paris (14th)

1913 – (SNBA) 340 - Femme à la robe mauve.
341 - Fanny et Floc.

1914 – (SNBA) 314 - Sur le balcon.
315 - Bleu et orange.

1919 – (SNBA) 1786 - Portrait de Mme D. B...
1787 - La robe bleue.
1788 - Intérieur.

1920 – (SNBA) 389 - Portrait de Mlle M. A.
390 - Jeune fille au chat.
391 - Intérieur.

Amis des arts. 64ᵉ expo. Elève de MM. R… et Frinel, 18 rue Boissonade, Paris (14th)

1920 – (BORDEAUX) 164 - Intérieur (2000 fr)
165 - Enfant lisant (500 fr)

Amis des arts. 65ᵉ expo. Elève de R.-X. Prinet. Société nationale des Beaux-Arts : A. A Paris, 18 rue Boissonade, Paris (14th)

1921 – (BORDEAUX) 178 - Intérieur (2500 fr)
179 - Nature morte (1000 fr)

1921 – (SNBA) 348 - Intérieur.
349 - Jeune femme à la parure.
350 - Intérieur.
351 - Portrait de Mlle D. F….
1273 - Panneau Pétunias et raisins (gouache)

1922 – (SNBA) 272 - Portrait de la famille D...
273 - Intérieur.
274 - Intérieur.
275 - Nature morte (anémones).
1080 - Phlox et pommes (gouache).

Amis des arts. 66ᵉ expo. Elève de R.-X. Prinet. Société nationale des Beaux-Arts : A. A Paris, 18 rue Boissonade, Paris (14th)

1922 – (BORDEAUX) 159 – Intérieur (500 fr)
160 - Etude de Maisons (400 fr)

Galerie Georges Petit. 10ème exposition de la Cimaise. Galerie Devambez, 45 boulevard Malesherbes, .8 - 30 December 1922. 18 rue Boissonade, Paris (14th)

1922 – 96 - Intérieur (Tempera)
97 - Jeune fille au chat (Tempera)
98 - Fleurs (Tempera)
99 - La porte verte (Tempera)

Galerie Devambez. La Cimaise. 11ᵉ exposition. 18 rue Boissonade, Paris (14th)

1923 – 30 - Intérieur (Tempera)
31 - Fleurs (phlox) (Tempera)

	32 - Portrait d'une jeune femme (Tempera)
	33 - Venise (étude) (oil)
	34 - Chambéry (étude) (Tempera).
	35 - Intérieur (oil)
	36 - Fleurs (oil)
	37 - Eglise de la Salute, Venise (oil)

Amis des arts. 67e expo. Elève de R.-X. Prinet. Société Nationale des Beaux-Arts : A. A Paris, 18 rue Boissonade, Paris (14th)

1923 – (BORDEAUX)	190 – Intérieur (850 fr)
	191 - Fauteuil rose (850 fr)
1923 – (TUILERIES)	253 - Intérieur.
	254 - Intérieur.
	255 - Portrait.
	256 - Fleurs.
1924 – (TUILERIES)	409 - Intérieur.
	410 - Intérieur.
	411 - Etude.
	411 bis - Intérieur.
1925 – (TUILERIES)	420 - Intérieur (le lit orange).
	421 - Les fauteuils bleus.
	422 - Intérieur.
	423 - Nature morte.
	424 - Nature morte.
1926 – (TUILERIES)	493 - L'intérieur.
	494 - Jour de soleil.
	495 - Femme au canapé.
	496 - Nature morte.
	497 - ----

Amis des arts. 70ème expo. Elève de R. X. Prinet. Société nationale des Beaux-Arts : A. A Paris, 18 rue Boissonade, Paris (14th)

1926 – (BORDEAUX)	238 - Sur le balcon (3000 fr)
	239 - Intérieur (2000 fr)
1927 – (TUILERIES)	578 - Intérieur.
	579 - ----

	580 - Enfants au jardin.
	581 - Etude.
	582 - ----
1928 – (TUILERIES)	724 - Enfant au soleil.
	725 - Peinture.
	726 - ----
	727 - ----
	728 - ----
1929 – (TUILERIES)	353 - Chrysanthèmes.
	354 - Nature morte.
1930 – (TUILERIES)	731 - Intérieur.
	732 - Intérieur.
	733 - Fleurs.
	734 - Peinture.
1931 – (TUILERIES)	381 - Intérieur.
	382 - Intérieur.
	383 - Intérieur.
	384 - Fleurs.
1932 – (AUTOMNE)	366 - Intérieur.
	367 - Nature morte.
1932 – (TUILERIES)	466 - Peinture.
	467 - Peinture.
1933 – (SNBA)	624 - Intérieur.
	625 - Nature morte.
	626 - Nature morte.
	627 - Peinture.
1933 – (AUTOMNE)	395 - Intérieur.
	396 - Fleurs.
1933 – (TUILERIES)	645 - Peinture.
	646 - Nature morte.
	647 - Nature morte.
1934 – (SNBA)	576 - Intérieur.
	577 - Intérieur.
	578 - Intérieur.
	579 - Fleurs.

1934 – (TUILERIES) 545 - Intérieur.
546 - Intérieur.
547 - Intérieur.
1935 – (SNBA) 493 - Intérieur.
494 - Nature morte.
495 - Nature morte.
496 - Paysage.
497 - Paysage.
1935 – (TUILERIES) 479 - Intérieur.
480 - Intérieur.
481 - Paysage.

40 rue Boissonade, Paris (14th)

1936 – (SNBA) 500 - Intérieur.
501 - Nature morte.
502 - Paysage.
1936 – (TUILERIES) 414 - Intérieur.
415 - Paysage.
416 - Nature morte.
1938 – (TUILERIES) 436 - Neige.
437 - Nature morte.
1939 – (TUILERIES) 403 - Nature morte.

DAVIES David

Born 21 May 1864 Ballarat, Australia, died 26 March 1939 Looe, Cornwall, G.B..

2 rue d'Odessa, hôtel Saint-Malo, chez M. Altson, Paris (14th)

1893 – (SNBA) 313 – *'Marine'.*

DEGEN Mary

Born Sydney, Australia.

3 quai Malaquais, Paris, (6th)

1911 – (INDEPENDANTS) 1676 - Femme au miroir.
1677 - Tête de jeune fille.
1678 - Tulipes.
1679 - Traits sur nappe blanche.
1680 - Anémones.
1681 - Portrait.

15 quai de Bourbon, Paris, (4th)

1912 – (INDEPENDANTS)	854 - Ève.
	855 - Portrait.
	856 - Portrait.
1913 – (INDEPENDANTS)	3218 - Fantaisie orientale.

15 quai de Bourbon, Paris (4th)

1913 – (SNBA)	354 - L'île heureuse.
1914 – (SNBA)	323 - En Arcadie.

DEND Vera Helen

Born Australia.

18 impasse du Maine, Paris (14th)

1913 – (AUTOMNE)	484 - Au soleil.

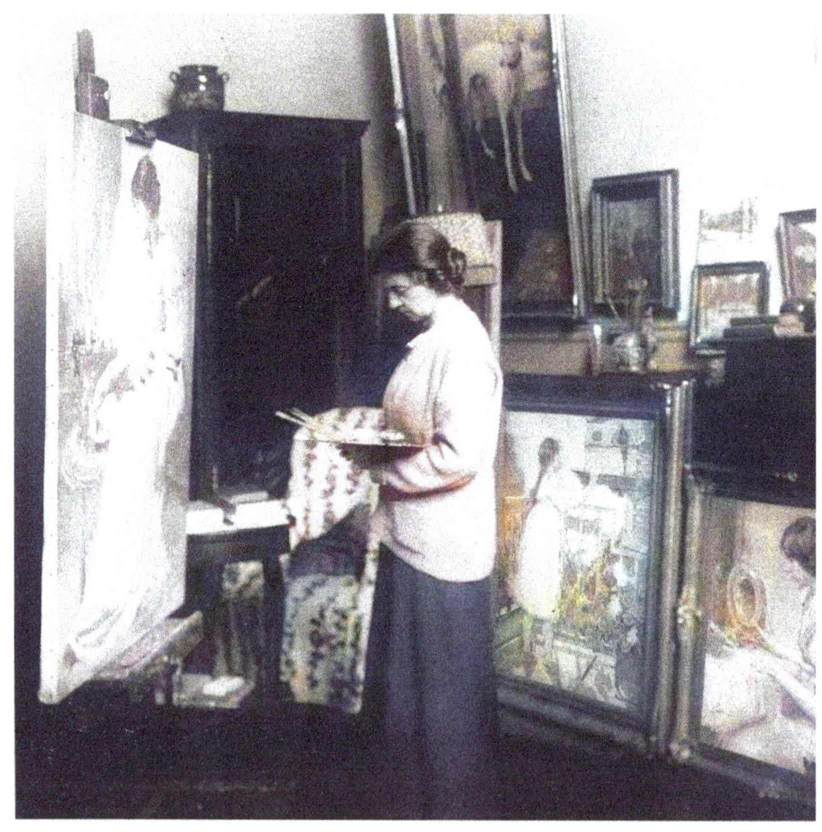

Bessie Davidson in her studio at rue Boissonade, Paris 1913.

F

FARMER John

Born 1 June 1897 Melbourne, Australia, died 29 April 1989.

2 rue Bonaparte, American Arts, Paris (6th)

1924 – (AUTOMNE)	621 - Nature morte.
	622 - Le vase bleu.

5 rue Barrault, Paris (13th)

1933 – (SNBA)	812 - Glaïeuls.
	813 - Portrait d'homme.
	814 - Nature morte.

FERN Emily Isabel

Born 1881 Ballarat, Australia; died 1953 Johannesburg.

34 rue d'Alésia, Paris (14th)

1934 – (SNBA)	794 - Portrait.
1934 – (TUILERIES)	739 - Portrait.
	740 - Portrait.

FOX : see **CARRICK-FOX** Ethel

FOX Emanuel Philipps

Born 12 March 1865 Melbourne, Australia, died 8 October 1915 Melbourne.

Elève de MM. Bougeureau, T. Robert-Fleury et Gérôme. 86, rue Notre-Dame-des-Champs, Paris (6th)

1890 – (SAF)	959 - Tricoteuse.
	960 - Automne.

Rue des Beaux-Arts, hôtel de Nice, Paris (6th)

1891 – (SAF)	646 - Convalescente.
	647 - Veuve.
1894 – (SAF)	758 - Portrait (médaille de 3ème classe)
	759 - Portrait de ma cousine.

65 boulevard Arago, Paris (13th)

1906 – (SNBA)	491 - Une histoire d'amour.
	492 - Dame en blanc.
	493 - Rêverie.

1907 – (SNBA) 467- Al fresco.
468 - Le travail.

21 rue Bréa, chez Paul Foinet, Paris (6th)

1908 – (SNBA) 432 - Dans le jardin.

65 boulevard Arago, Paris (13th)

1909 – (SNBA) 447 - Jeune femme en blanc.
448 - Effet de nuit.
449 - Etude.

1910 – (SNBA) 490 - Mère et enfants.
491 - Lever de la lune Australie.
492 - La Tonnelle.
493 - Etude de Nu.

1911 – (SNBA) 527 - Les étudiantes.
528 - Portrait de Miss Gérard Anderson.
529 - Repos.
530 - Venise. (App. à M. Herbert Daly.)
531 - La toilette.
532 - Tête d'une femme.

21e expo. Société des Amis des arts de Nantes. 2 Feb. – 17 March 1912. 65 bd Arago, Paris (13th)

1912 – (NANTES) 169 - Femme nue (1000 fr)
170 - Noir et blanc (600 fr)

1912 – (AUTOMNE) 588 - L'Eté.
589 - Nu en plein air.

1912 – (SNBA) 538 - Le thé.
539 - La tonnelle.
540 - L'heure du bain.
541 - Le bac.
542 - Déjeuner.
543 - Château Gaillard.

Galerie Georges Petit. 30ème exposition de la Société internationale de Peinture & Sculpture. 6-31 December 1912. 65 boulevard Arago, Paris (13th)

1912 – 44 - Fin d'un roman.
45 - Le Miroir.

46 - Sur le Balcon.
47 - Vue en plein air.
48 - Repos.
49 - Portrait.

1913 : Peinture. 65 boulevard Arago, Paris (13th)

1913 – (SOCIETE DES PEINTRES ORIENTALISTES)
Bou-Saâda, Algérie :

292 - Un jardin.
293 - Le fleuve.
294 - Entrée de la ville.
295 - La rue principale.
296 - Boutiques sur la place.
297 - Jour de marché.
298 - Une rue.
299 - Entrée de la ville, le soir.
300 - La place.
301 - Autour de la fontaine.
302 - Vue de Tanger.
303 - La baie à Tanger.
304 - Cadix (Espagne).
305 - Une rue à Cadix.
306 - Le Guadalquivir , Cordoba.
307 - Vue de Cordoba (Espagne).

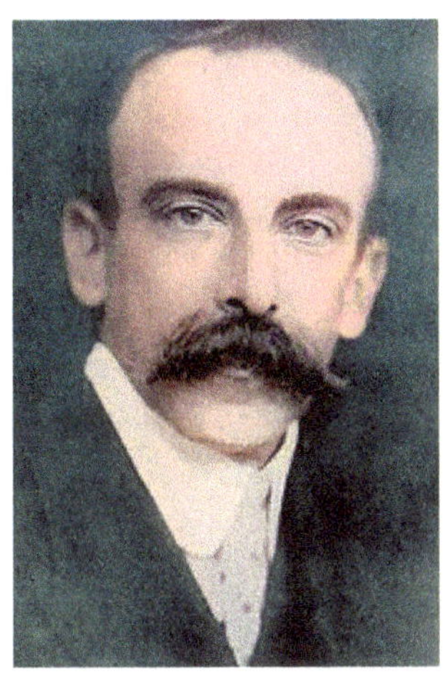

E. Phillips Fox

1920 – (SNBA) 490 - Repos.
491 - Femme nue.
492 - Blanc et noir.

FREEMAN Madge
Born 1895 Bendigo, Victoria, Australia, died Ivanhoe, Victoria 1970.

4, rue Belloni, Paris (15th)

1925 – (TUILERIES) 720 - Nature morte.
721 - Nature morte.

FRICKE Olive Alice
Born Ballarat, Victoria, Australia

3, rue Paul-Sauniere, chez Mlle Pitt, Paris (16th)

1928 – (SNBA) 769 - Le chale chinois.
770 - Nature morte.

FRY Edith or Edith May
Born 1883 Copeland, NSW, died 1950.

31 Carlingford Road, London G.B.

1924 – (INDEPENDANTS) 1164bis - Dans l'atelier (7500 fr)

31 Upper Brook Street, London G.B.

1925 – (INDEPENDANTS) 1273 - La terrasse (7500 fr)

4 the Mell, Parkhill Road, London G.B.

1926 – (INDEPENDANTS) 1293 - Château d'Allières (5000 fr)
1294 - Jardin anglais (2500 fr).

FULLER Florence Ada
Born 1867 Port-Elisabeth, South Africa, died 17 July 1946 Gladesville, NSW.

Elève de MM. Bouguereau et Ferrier. 13 avenue de la Grande-Armée, Paris

1895 – (SAF) 2395 - Étude (pastel)

Elève de MM. Raphaël Collin et Paul Leroy. 49 boulevard du Montparnasse, Paris

1896 – (SAF) 851 - Portrait de Mme...
852 - Une rue de village.

Elève de M. R. Collin. Lawnside, Sow-Park, Newport, Mon, G.B.

1897 – (SAF) 681 - *Travail d'été ; fille à la brouette*

Elève de MM. Raphaël Collin et Paul Leroy. 7 rue Chabanais, Paris, chez MM. Lorne et Hans.

1897 – (SAF) 854 - Portrait Of Mme Collin
1897 – (SNBA) La Gianeuse.

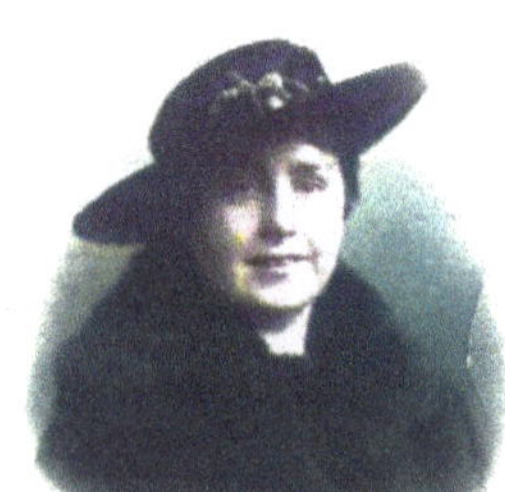

Florence Fuller.

G

GEACH Portia

Born 24 December 1873 Melbourne; died 5 October 1959 Sydney.

71 Cornhill, c/o Union Bank of Australia, London G.B.

1926 – (SNBA) 519 - The Negress.

GIBSON Mlle Bessie (Elizabeth Dixon)

Born 16 May 1868 Ipswich, Queensland, Australia, died 13 July 1961 Brisbane, Queensland.

8 bis, rue Campagne-Première, Paris (14th)

Galerie Georges Petit. Société de la Miniature, de l'Aquarelle et des arts précieux. 22 Jan – 2 Feb 1910. Elève de Mmes Debillemont-Chardon et Laforge. 27 avenue du Maine, Paris (14th)

1910 –

146 - Étude en gris.

147 - En robe de cardinal.

148 - Portrait de Mlle M. D…

149 - Jeune Algérienne.

150 - Portrait d'un petit garçon.

151 - Étude d'une petite fille.

152 - La Dame à l'éventail.

153 - Étude de profil.

154 - Une femme Italienne.

155 - La Pensée triste.

156 - Elisabeth d'Autriche, reine de France, d'après Clouet.

157 - Master Hare, d'après Reynolds.

Galerie Georges Petit. Société de la Miniature, de l'Aquarelle et des arts précieux. 22 Jan – 2 Feb 1911. 9 rue Campagne-Première, Paris (14th)

1911 –

139 - Portrait de Mme Mac C…

140 - Portrait de M. de X…

141 - Portrait étude de M. S…

142 - Jeune fille en kimono.

143 - Vieille femme.

	144 - Parsons's daughter, d'après Romney.
	145 - Portrait d'homme, d'après Lawrence.
	146 - Lucie.
	147 - Un cadre contenant : Etude de nu. Petite Bretonne. Miniatures sur ivoire.
1920 – (SAF)	732 - Petite Andrée.
	733 - Le pot bleu.
1921 – (SAF)	873 – 'Ninette'.
	874 – 'Intérieur'.
1921 – (AUTOMNE)	913 - Intérieur.
1922 – (SDAI)	1476 - Notre-Dame, vue de la Seine.
	1477 - Nature morte.
	1478 - Le Panthéon.
1922 –(SAF)	779 - Portrait de Jeanne.
	780 - Intérieur.
1922 – (AUTOMNE)	1002 - Portrait de Mlle W...
	1003 - Portrait.
	1004 - Intérieur.
1923 – (SAF)	764 - Portrait de M. le colonel de G...
	765 - Le bonnet blanc.
	766 - Nature morte.
1923 – (AUTOMNE)	739 - Le Collier bleu.
1924 – (SDAI)	1274 - Portrait (2000 fr)
	1275 - Le dessert (1000 fr)
1924 – (SAF)	864 - Portrait.
	865 - Nature morte.
1924 – (AUTOMNE)	738 - La Toile.
1925 – (SDAI)	1365 - Echarpe rayée. (1000 fr)
	1366 - Nature morte. (800 fr)
1925 – (SAF)	461 - Portrait.
(SAF)	300 - Le dessert.
1925 – (AUTOMNE)	508 - Sur le quai à Honfleur.

1926 – (SAF)	861 - Portrait de Mlle Horatia Wardlan. (mention honorable)
	862 - Portait de Mlle Crawhall.
1927 – (SAF)	821 - Portrait.
	822 - Le bas gris.
1927 – (AUTOMNE)	893 - Le Reflet.
	894 - La Toilette.
1928 – (SAF)	886 - Portrait de Miss K...
	887 - Portrait.
1928 – (AUTOMNE)	758 - Le petit pot marron (design).
	759 - Sur la Seine (design).
1929 – (SAF)	1000 - Portrait de miss Somerset.
	1001 - La robe rouge.
1930 – (SAF)	929 - Rouge, blanc et bleu.
	930 - Profil de vieillard.
1930 – (AUTOMNE)	912 - Le collier bleu (design).
1931 – (SAF)	994 - Portrait de Miss Osbourne-Williams.
	995 - L'Enigme.
1932 – (SAF)	1070 - Jeune femme en rose pâle (illustration).
	1071 - A la fenêtre.
1932 – (SDAI)	1592 - Fleurs. (1000 fr)
	1593 - Fleurs. (600 fr)
1933 – (TUILERIES)	984 - Aux temps des boucles.
	985 - Fleurs.
1933 – (SAF)	1083 - Mère et bébé (illustration).
1933 – (AUTOMNE)	640 - Intérieur (design).
1934 – (TUILERIES)	833 – 'Fleurs'.
	834 – 'Fleurs'.
	835 – Croquis de nu.

1934 – *Saint-Quentin : XIIIe Exposition des Beaux-Arts. Société des Amis des Arts de Saint-Quentin et de l'Aisne. 14 April – 6 May*

436 – Intérieur, aquarelle.
437 – Fleurs blanches, peinture.
438 – Fleurs jaunes, peinture.

1934 – (SAF)	1084 - Lucette et son panier de fleurs
	1085 - Fleurs
1934 – (AUTOMNE)	629 - Tête de femme (design).
1935 – (TUILERIES)	766 - Rouge et blanc.
	767 - Nu.
	768 - Fleurs.
	769 - Saint-Marco, à Venise.
	770 - Marché aux fleurs.
1935 – (SAF)	1010 - La redingote verte.
	1011 - Le dessert.
1936 – (TUILERIES)	699 - Fleurs.
	700 - Les Soucis.
	701 - Le Porche blanc.
1936 – (SAF)	1098 - Profil de jeune femme.
	1099 - Pot de fleurs.
1937 – (SAF)	579 - L'ombre d'un chapeau.
1938 – (TUILERIES)	709 - Fleurs.
	710 - Nature morte.
	711 - Pivoine blanche.
	712 - Le soir à Honfleur.
	713 - Panthéon.
1938 – (SAF)	698 - Portrait de Mme May.
	699 - Fleurs.
1939 – (SAF)	1292 - Portrait.
	1293 - Fleurs.
	1294 - Nature morte.

GOLDIE Charles Frederick
Born 1870 Auckland, New Zealand, died 1947 Auckland, NZ.

et chez James Bourlet et Fils, London G.B.

1936 – (SAF)	1129 - Le sommeil.
	1130 - Il fait lourd.
1938 – (SAF)	716 - In Dreamland.
	717 - A Midsummer's day.
1939 – (SAF)	1324 - Thoughts of a Tohunga.
	1325 - In Doubt (Atama Paparangi).

GONINAN Alfreda
Born Newcastle, New South Wales, Australia.

7 rue Léopold-Robert, Paris (14th)

1921 – (AUTOMNE) 957 - Nature morte.

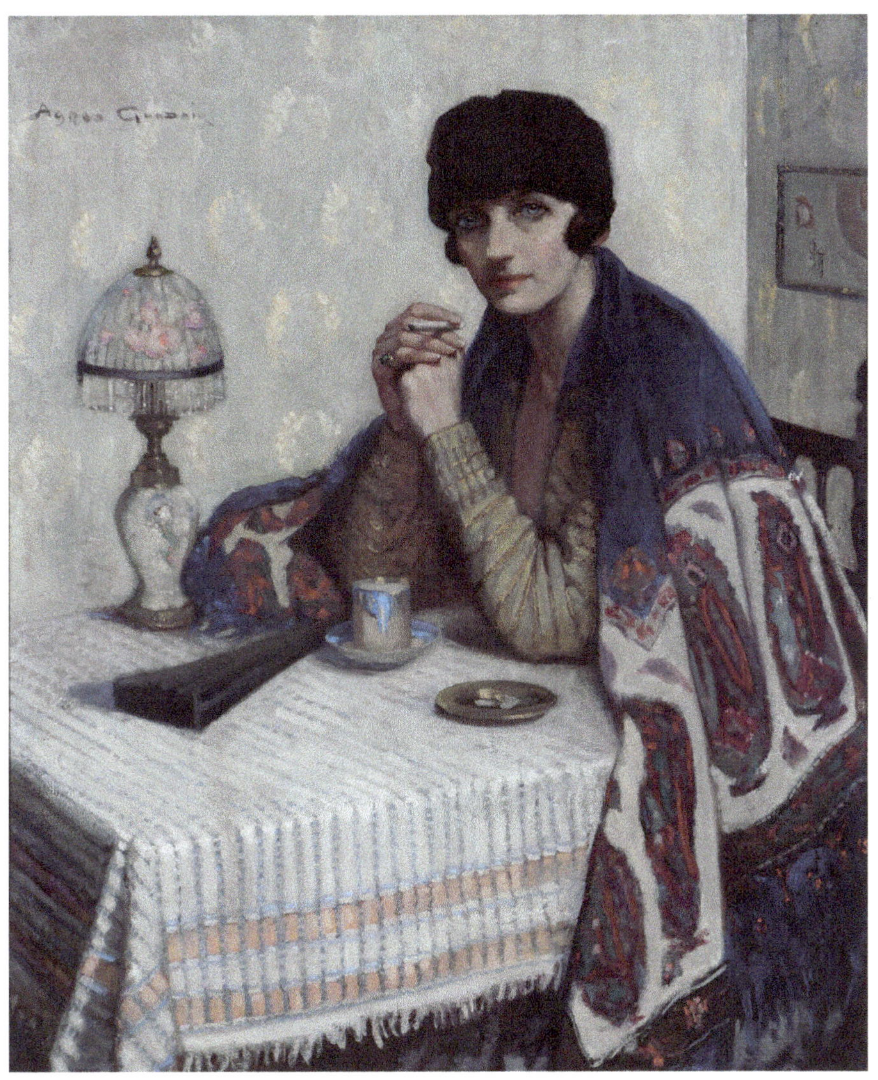

Agnes Goodsir: *Girl with Cigarette,* c. 1925
Oil on Canvas, Bendigo Art Gallery

GOODHART Joseph Christian

Born 1875 Adelaide; died 1962 Victor Harbour, South Australia.

1929 – (SAF) 4407 - The poppet head (gravure)

4408 – Klondyke (gravure)

GOODSIR Agnes or Agnes-Noyes

Born 1864 Portland, Victoria, Australia, died 1939 Paris, France.

Elève de MM. Raphaël Collin, Courtois et Prinet. 7 rue Léopold-Robert, Paris (14th)

1902 – (SAF) 733 - Portrait.

734 - Intérieur.

Elève de MM. Collin, Courtois et J.-P. Laurens. 18 rue de Mila, Paris (9th)

1903 – (SAF) 808 - Portrait de Mlle S...

8 boulevard Edgard-Quinet, Paris (14th)

1905 – (SNBA) 572 - La lettre.

573 - Réflexions.

chez M. Lefebvre-Foinet, 2 rue Brea, Paris (6th)

1906 – (SNBA) 572 - Le collet rouge.

19 rue Vavin, chez M. Lefebvre-Foinet, Paris (6th)

1907 – (SNBA) 534 - Désillusionnée.

52 Sutherland Avenue, London G.B.

1912 – (INDEPENDANTS) 1369 - Pendant le repos.

1370 - Louise.

1371 - L'éventail blanc.

18 rue de l'Odéon (5th)

1921 – (SNBA) 534 - Le Chapeau bleu.

535 - Cherry.

1922 – (SNBA) 432 - Femme à la cigarette.

433 - Femme au ruban noir.

434 - Coin du Salon.

435 - Intérieur.

1922 – (SDAI) 1531 - La lettre.

1532 - Louise.

1533 - Étude.

1923 – (SNBA) 834 – 'Cherry'.

835 - Liseuse dans un intérieur.

	836 - Intérieur.
1924 – (SNBA)	420 - La jupe chinoise.
	421 - Femme au canapé.
	422 - Au sixième.
1924 – (SDAI)	1307 - Le salon bleu (1200 fr)
	1308 - Le petit déjeuner. (1200 fr)
1925 – (SNBA)	179 - Les Sœurs.
1925 – (SDAI)	1419 - Intérieur d'atelier. (1800 fr)
	1420 - Intérieur. (1200 fr)
1926 – (SNBA)	537 - La lettre.
	538 - L été.
	539 - Portrait du Comte Léon Tolstoï.
	540 - Portrait de l'artiste.
	541 - Portrait de Mme Rachel Dunn.

Rétrospective '30 ans d'art indépendant : 1884-1914'.

1926 – (SDAI)	1083 – Neurasthénie (1911).
	1084 - Arc de Triomphe (1912).
	1085 - Anémones (1913).
	1086 - Femme au peignoir (1922).
	1087 - Le salon (1924).
	1088 - Femme en chemise (1924).
1928 – (SNBA)	837 - Portrait de Mlle Rose Le Quesne.
	838 - Portrait de M. le Colonel Whyte.
	839 - Femme à la cigarette.
	840 - Le petit déjeûner.
	841 - Le peignoir rose.
1929 – (SNBA)	778 - Lassitude d'esprit.
	779 - Un type du Quartier Latin.
	780 - Le Ménage quotidien.
	781 - Intérieur d'atelier.
	782 - Nature morte.
1930 – (SNBA)	852 - La Lettre.
	853 - Portrait de Mlle R. Petroncini, nièce du comte Manzoni, ambassadeur à Paris.

854 - Dans un café, quartier latin.
855 - Portrait.
856 - Nature morte.

1931 – (SNBA) 972 - Le Collier de jade.
973 - Un nu, 1930.
974 - Le petit déjeuner.
975 - Nature morte, bleu et or.
976 - Nature morte, rose pâle et bleu.

1932 – (SNBA) 904 - Portrait de la Princesse K. D.
905 - Une corbeille de fruits.
906 - Chrysanthèmes.
907 - Myosotis.

1934 – *Saint-Quentin : XIIIe Exposition des Beaux-Arts. Société des Amis des Arts de Saint-Quentin et de l'Aisne. 14 April – 6 May*
466 - Nature morte, peinture.
467 - Roses, peinture.
468 - Fleurs, peinture.

Galerie Georges Petit. Société internationale des Femmes Peintres & Sculpteurs. 6 – 17 July 1934

1934 – 88 - Le Chapeau noir.
89 - L'estampe japonaise.
90 - Myosotis.

1934 – (SNBA) 900 - Nature morte et fleurs.
901 - Nature morte.
902 - Fleurs.
903 - Nature morte.
904 - La Première Communion.

1935 – (SNBA) 792 - Femme vue de dos.
793 - Le jardin de sommeil.
794 - Dans un atelier.
795 - Cherry.
796 - Les glaïeuls.

GREEN Anne Alison, or Annie

Born 1878 Bridport, Dorset, G.B., died Brisbane, Australia 1954.

15, rue Campagne-Première, Paris (14th)

1920 – (SNBA) 14. Portrait.

15. Le Port.
16. Portrait "Elise".

1923 – (SNBA) 12. Portrait of Mme N...
13. Portrait.
14. Portrait.

1924 – (SNBA) 17. Portrait.
18. Mme C...

1925 – (SNBA) 7. Portrait.

GRIER Edmund Wyly
Born 26 November 1862 Melbourne, Australia, died 7 December 1957 Toronto, Ontario.

Elève de MM. Bouguereau, Robert-Fleury et Legros. 6 rue de l'Arrivée, Paris (6th)

1885 – (SAF) 3787 – ' Suspense' (bas-relief, cire).

Elève de MM. Bouguereau et T. Robert-Fleury. Saint Ives, Cornwall G.B.

1890 – (SAF) 1109 - Bereft.
(médaille de 3ème classe)

GRIER Louis Monro
Born 1864 Melbourne, Australia, died 1920 St Ives, Cornwall. G.B.

Elève de MM. Bouguereau et T. Robert-Fleury. Saint Ives, Cornwall

1891 – (SAF) 753 - La garde de nuit ; - pêcheurs de la Cornouaille gardant leurs filets.
(médaille de 3ème classe)

St Ives, Cornwall G.B, et 14 rue Gaillon, chez M. Pottier, Paris (2nd)

1896 – (SAF) 950 - *Dans les Pays-Bas.*

GRUNER Elioth Lauritz Leganyer
Born 16 December 1882 Gisborne, New Zealand, died 17 October 1939 Sydney, Australia.

1928 - (SNBA) 5 oil paintings, catalogue not found.

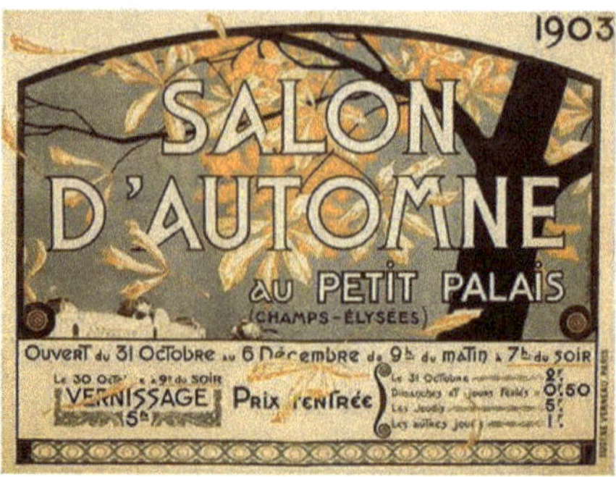
1903
SALON
D'AUTOMNE
au PETIT PALAIS
(CHAMPS-ÉLYSÉES)
Ouvert du 31 Octobre au 6 Décembre de 9h du matin à 7h du soir
VERNISSAGE
5h
Prix d'entrée
2f.
0f.50
5f.
1f.

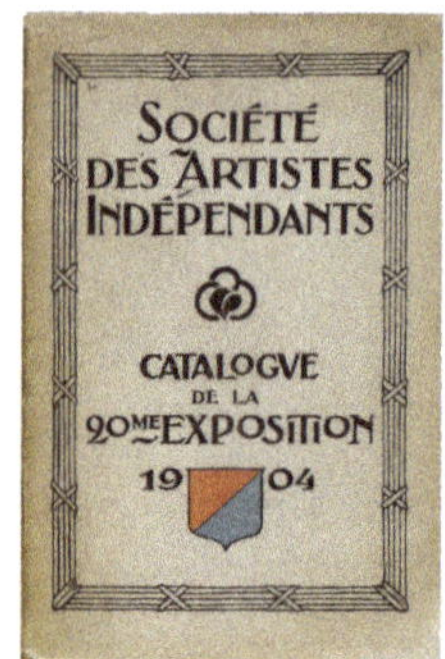
SOCIÉTÉ
DES ARTISTES
INDÉPENDANTS
CATALOGVE
DE LA
20ME EXPOSITION
19 04

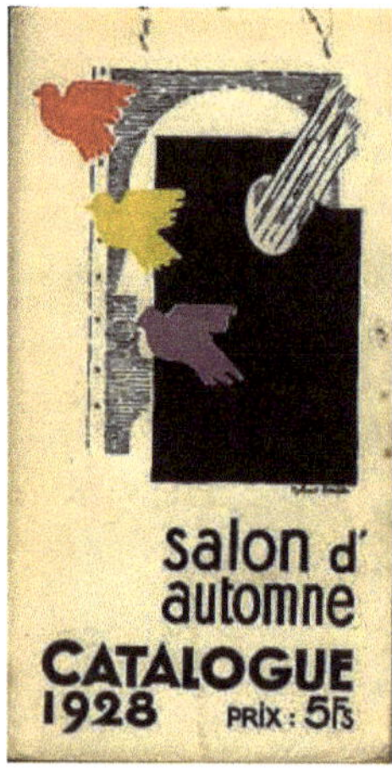
salon d'
automne
CATALOGUE
1928
PRIX : 5Frs

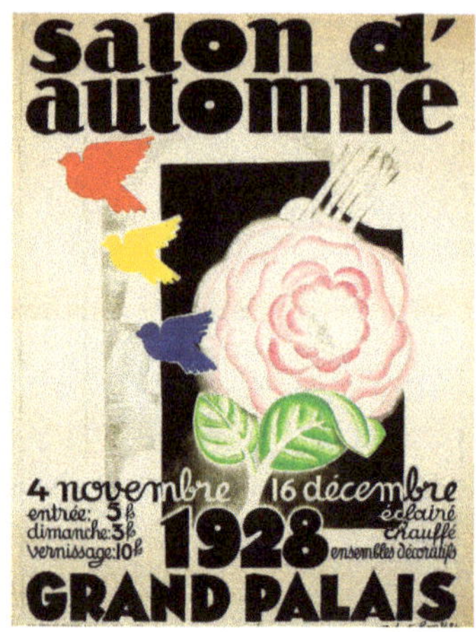
salon d'
automne
4 novembre 16 décembre
entrée: 5f
dimanche: 3f
vernissage: 10f
1928
éclairé
chauffé
ensembles décoratifs
GRAND PALAIS

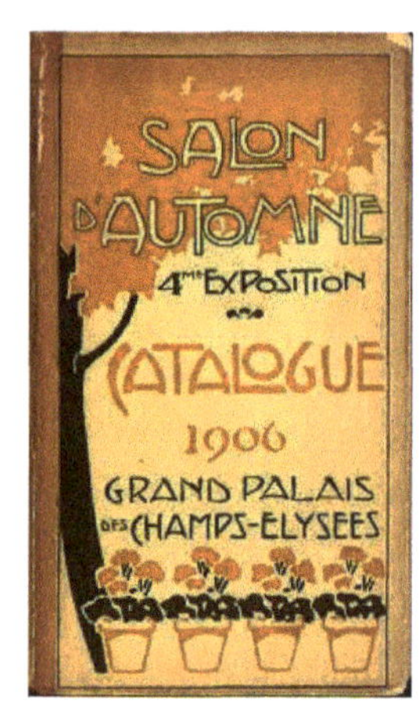
SALON
D'AUTOMNE
4me EXPOSITION
CATALOGUE
1906
GRAND PALAIS
DES CHAMPS-ELYSEES

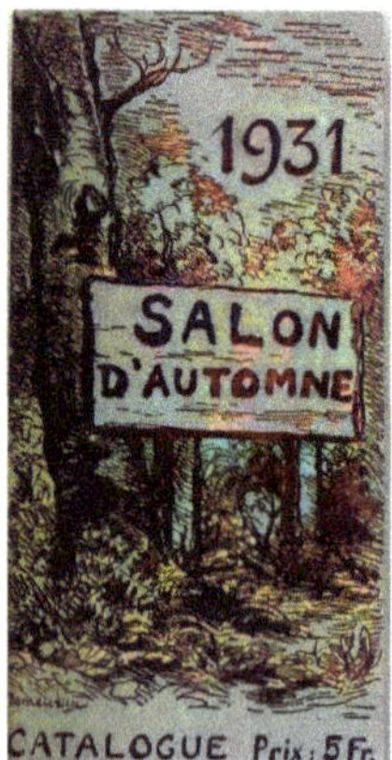
1931
SALON
D'AUTOMNE
CATALOGUE Prix: 5Fr.

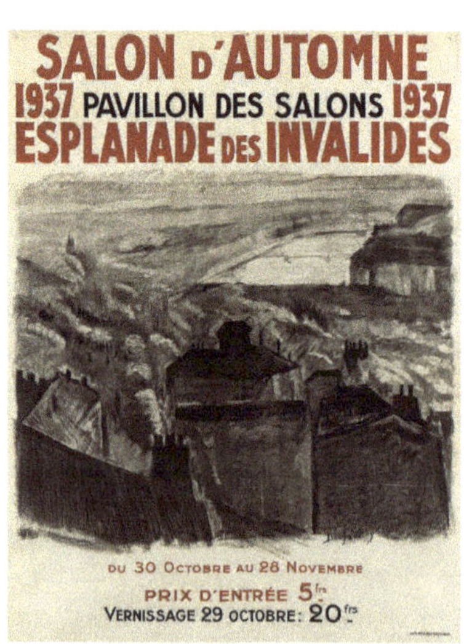
SALON D'AUTOMNE
1937 PAVILLON DES SALONS 1937
ESPLANADE DES INVALIDES
DU 30 OCTOBRE AU 28 NOVEMBRE
PRIX D'ENTRÉE 5frs
VERNISSAGE 29 OCTOBRE: 20frs

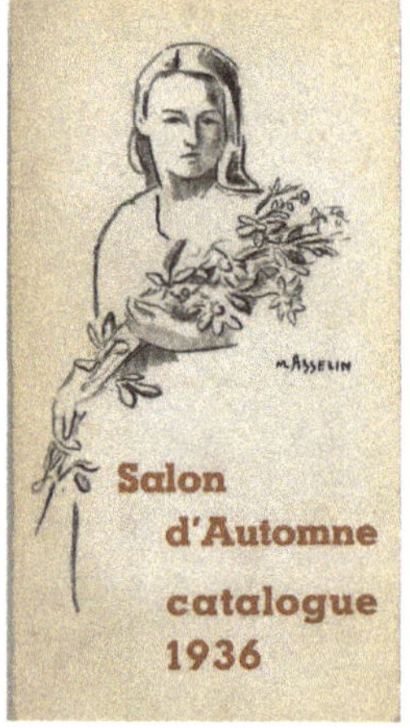
M. ASSELIN
Salon
d'Automne
catalogue
1936

H

HALES Samuel

Born Dunedin, New Zealand 1868, died London 1953.

Elève de M. Marcel Baschet. 52 avenue du Maine, Paris (14th)

1897 – (SAF) 809 - La nuit.

Elève de Doucet et de M. Marcel Baschet. 52 Avenue du Maine, Paris (14th)

1898 – (SAF) 991 - Marine.

HALLEN Ambrose Lancelot

Born 1887 Parramatta, NSW, died 1942.

225 rue d'Alésia, Paris (14th)

1926 – (INDEPENDANTS) 1611 - Tartane italienne (550 fr)
1612 - Aquarelle (330 fr)

1927 – (INDEPENDANTS) 1677 - Ondarroa (Espagne) (2500 fr)
1678 - Yarmouth (île de Wight) (1500 fr)

1928 – (INDEPENDANTS) 1939 - Femme canaque,
Appartient à l'auteur.
1940 - Rêverie fantastique ,
Appartient à l'auteur.

1929 – (INDEPENDANTS) 2058 - Solitude (1500 fr)
2059 - Femme lisant (1500 fr)

HAMPEL Carl

Born 1887 Bendigo, Victoria, died 1942 London.

175 Adelaide Road, London, G.B.

1936 – (SAF) 1221 - Tulips and Lilac.

1937 – (SAF) 633 - Portrait of Madame R. W.
1608 - Hiver.

HANSEN Theo Brooke

Born 1870 Melbourne, died 1935 Melbourne.

Elève de MM. J.-P. Laurens et Benjamin-Constant. 6 rue Delambre, hôtel de la Tourelle, Paris (14th)

1895 – (SAF) 916 - Fatigué.
917 - Jeune fille.

HARRISON Eleanor. Ritchie, or **HARRISON**, E. Ritchie
Born 1854 Victoria, Australia, died 1895.

Elève de MM. Collin et Courtois. 13 rue Boissonade, Paris (14th)

1886 – (SAF) 1170 - La mère Honoré.

Elève de MM. Krug et Collin. 20 rue Jacob, chez M. Chabod, Paris (6th)

1887 – (SAF) 1179 - Portrait d'une dame australienne.
1180 - Une 'matelotte' d'Etaples.

Elève de MM. Feyen-Perrin, Krug et R. Collin. Etaples, Pas-de-Calais, France.

1888 – (SAF) 1268 - Au temps des cerises.

HAZSARD Rhona
Born 21 January 1901 Thames, New Zealand, died 21 February 1931 Alexandria, Egypt.

Rue Castel-de-Chierry, Château-Thierry, Aisne, France.

1927 – (SAF) 931 - Sardiniers (Bretagne).

HODGKINS Frances Mary
Born 28 April 1869 Dunedin, New Zealand , died 13 May 1947 Dorchester, Dorset G.B.

Galerie Georges Petit. 2ème exposition - Société internationale d'aquarellistes. 16 – 30 Nov1906.

1906 – 85 - Le Ballon rouge.
86 - La Petite Marie.
87 - Le Pont Blanc.
88 - Le Rialto (Venise).
89 - Les Voiles séchant.

Galerie Georges Petit. 6ème exposition - Société internationale d'aquarellistes. 10 – 31 Oct 1910.

1910 – 213 - Avril.
214 - Le Déjeuner.
215 - Marie.
216 - L'Eté.
217 - Le Réveil.
218 - Les Pommes.

Galerie Georges Petit. 7ème exposition - Société internationale d'aquarellistes. 10 – 31 Oct 1911.

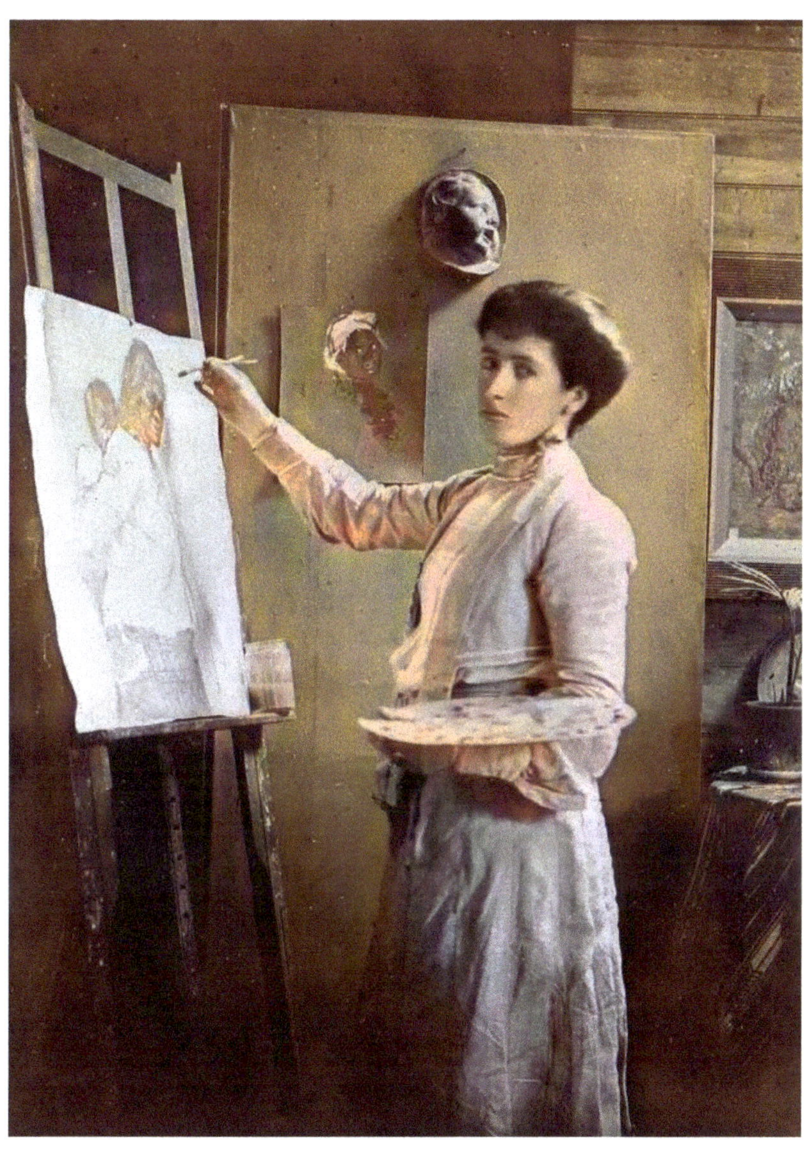

Frances Hodgkins in her studio in Wellington 1905, before leaving for Paris.

1911 – 221-228 Sur la plage.

Hôtel Belle-Vue, Montreuil-sur-Mer, France.

1924 – (AUTOMNE) 885 - Les Zinguers.

886 - Nature morte.

887 - Marché aux fleurs, Nice (aquarelle)

888 - Marché aux fleurs, Nice (aquarelle)

889 - Tête d'une jeune fille (aquarelle)

890 - Jeune femme (design).

891 - Jeune femme (design).

1a King's Street, Galleries Alex Reid et Lefebvre, Saint James, London G.B..

1938 – (AUTOMNE) *Exposition 'L'art anglais indépendant contemporain'.*

1883 - Cut melons.

1884 - Ibiza harbour.

HONEY Constance Winifred

Born 1892 London, arrived 1895 Melbourne; died 27 December 1944 London G.B.

59 Oakley Street, Chelsea, London G.B.

1928 – (SNBA) 983 - Prince Charming.

HOOKEY Mabel

Born 29 January 1871 Rokeby, Tasmania, died 13 June 1953 Hobart, Tasmania.

17-18, Nassau Street, chez J. Bourlet and sons Ltd, London G.B.

1928 – (SAF) 1034 - The Yard.

1035 - The white gum tree.

HOPE Edith Aimée

Born 1870 Sydney, NSW, died 1942 Mants, G.B.

8 Kensington Studios Kelso Place, London G.B.

1908 – (SNBA) 2221 - Arbres à Montreuil (gravure)

14 Kensington Studios, Kelso Place, Kensington, London G.B.

1909 – (SAF) 4579 - Le pirate (lithographie).

1909 – (SNBA) 614 - Vendange à Torcello.

1910 – (SNBA) 674 - Le café Trois Etoiles.

1911 – (SNBA) 711 - The reed pipe, oil.

8 Saint Alban's Studios, Saint Alban's Road, Kensington, London G.B.

1912 – (SNBA) 703 - Sur le seuil.

10 Pembroke Studios, London G.B.

1913 – (SNBA) 634 - Sous la treille.

1914 – (SNBA) 592 - A London Fruit Stall.

44 Bedford Gardens, London G.B.

1923 – (SNBA) 888 - Le bébé et la grand-mère.

Steep, Petersfield, Byways, Hampshire G.B.

1933 – (SAF) 1255 - Dahlias (illustration).

1934 – (SAF) 1244 - The village street.

HORNEL Edward Atkinson

Born 1 July 1864 Bachhus Marsh, Victoria, died 30 June 1933 Kirkcudbright, Scotland.

136 Wellington street, Glasgow, Scotland.

1893 : 10ème Exposition des XX – Bruxelles.

1893 – (EXPOSITION DES XX)

1 - the Goatherd.

2 - the Cowherd.

3 - Butterflies. Appartient à W.Burrell.

4 - the Brook. Appartient à Herbert Mc Nair.

HURRY Mary Farmer "Polly"

Born 1883 Kyneton, Victoria, died 1963 Victoria

125 boulevard du Montparnasse, The Paris American Art Co., Paris (6th)

1932 – (SNBA) 1070 - Portrait de Mme Hole.

5 rue Barrault, Paris (13th)

1933 – (SNBA) 1128 - Portrait de Mme Peltier.

1129 - Portrait d'homme.

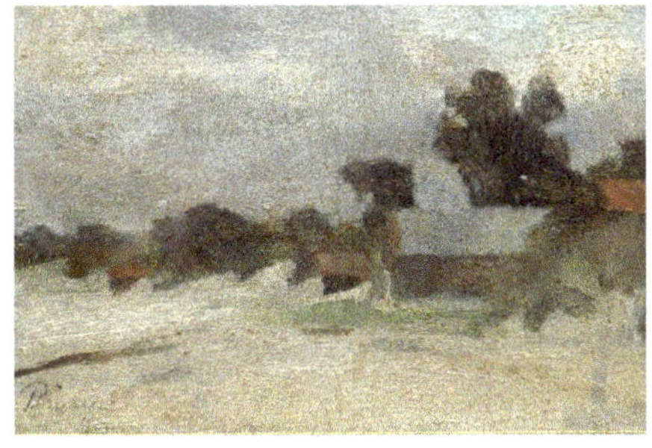

Polly Hurry: *Beach Scene,* 1927, oil on canvas.

J

JAMES C. Elizabeth
Born Victoria, Australia.
28 Glebe Place, Chelsea, London G.B.
1932 – (SAF) 1277 - Still Life.
1278 - The Falling tide Thames.

JENKINS, Constance Lillian
Born 29 June 1883 Melbourne, Victoria, died 1961 San Francisco, USA.
Elève de M.L. Bernard Hall, 18 rue Boissonade, Paris (14th)
1910 – (SAF) 1031 - Portrait

JOEL Grace Jane
Born 28 May 1865 Dunedin, NZ, died 6 March 1924 London G.B.
Elève de MM. Baschet et Schommer. 9 rue Campagne-Première, Paris (14th)
1901 – (SAF) 1095 – 'Son enfant'.
Elève de MM. Baschet et Schommer et Julian Academy. 60 Alexandra Road, Saint John's Wood, London G.B.
1903 – (SAF) 981 - Le retour par le sentier, crayon.
Elève de MM. Schommer et Baschet. Bank of New Zealand, Queen Victoria Street, London G.B.
1905 – (SAF) 1012 - Hollandaise.
Elève de MM. Baschet et Schommer. 7 Stanley Studios, Park Wall, London , G.B.
1908 – (SAF) 922 - Le grand-père d'Etaples.
923 - Enfants sans mère.
1909 – (SAF) 961 - Veuvage.
2414 - Les présages, aquarelle.
Elève de MM. Baschet et Schommer. 12 Milton-Chambers, 128 Cheyne Walk, London, G.B.
1910 – (SAF) 1037 - La Légende.
1911 – (SAF) 1004 - La fleur écarlate.
12 Milton Chambers, 128 Cheyne Walk, London, G.B.
1912 – (SAF) 956 - L'amour maternel.

1913 – (SAF) 969 - L'enfant adoré.
1921 – (SAF) 1040 - Portrait d'un musicien.
1923 – (SAF) 926 - Sympathie. (mention honorable)
1924 – (SAF) 1050 - La première séance.

JONES Marion

Born 1892 Bendigo, Victoria, died 1977 Melbourne, Victoria.

1 Carlyle Studio, 296 Kings Road, Chelsea, London G.B.

1923 – (SAF) 935 - Portrait of the Hon. W. Morris Hughes, Prime Minister of Australia.
1924 – (SAF) 1059 - Portrait de Miss Elma Rutledge.
1060 - Portrait of Baron de Belabre.
1928 – (SAF) 1106 - The Roman Shawl.
1929 – (SAF) 1238 - Portrait de Lord Novar.
1930 – (SAF) 1141 - Portrait of Miss Beryl Collins.
1935 – (SAF) 1223 - Portrait of Mrs Claude de Bernales, (illustration).

JORGENSEN Justus

Born 12 May 1893 Melbourne, Victoria, died 15 May 1975 Upper Fern Tree Gully, Victoria.

147 rue Broca, Paris (5th)

1925 – (SAF) 574 - Portrait de ma mère.
1925 – (AUTOMNE) 676 - Paysage en Australie.
677 - Sous le Pont des Arts.
1926 – (SAF) 1040 - Portrait de moi-même.

KELLY Anna Elizabeth, nee Abbott

Born in 12 April 1877 Christchurch, died 4 October Christchurch 1946

17 Nassau Street, chez Bourlet and Sons Ltd., London, G.B..

1932 – (SAF) 1339 - Portrait of Miss Edith Bryant. (mention honorable)
1340 - Portrait of Mrs Henry Crust. (illustration)
1933 – (SAF) 1361 - Miss Helen Buchanan.
1362 - Mrs Wilfred Sim. (illustration)

1934 – (SAF)	1334 - Miss Edith May. (médaille d'argent)
1935 – (SAF)	1261 - Miss Joan Cuningham.
	1262 - Toi toi Hinetavhara of the N'gati-Irekeku Tribe of Maoris.
1936 – (SAF)	1367 - Margaret Hatherley. (illustration)
1937 – (SAF)	702 - Ngaire Stevenson-Smith.
1938 – (SAF)	855 - Mrs Ernest Boulton.
	856 - Marg.
1939 – (SAF)	1608 - Lorna. (illustration)

KELLY Cecil Fletcher

Born 1878 Christchurch, NZ, died 1954 Christchurch, NZ.

17 Nassau Street, chez Bourlet and Sons Ltd, London G.B.

1935 – (SAF)	1263 - Lyttelton Harbour, New Zealand.
1937 – (SAF)	703 - Witch Hill, Rapaki, New-Zealand.

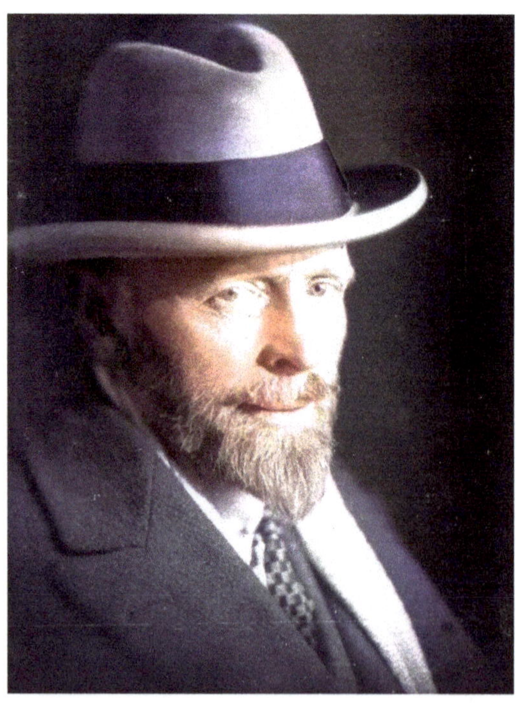

George Lambert, by May Moore, 1929.

L

LAMB Henry

Born 21 June 1883 Adelaide, South Australia, died 8 October 1960 Salisbury G.B.

9 Kensington Gate, London G.B.

Exposition 'L'art anglais indépendant contemporain'.

1938 – (AUTOMNE) 1895 - Felicia.

1896 - Miss Wardale.

LAMBERT George Washington

Born 13 September 1873 Saint Petersburg, Russia, died 29 May 1930 Camden, NSW.

31 boulevard Saint-Jacques, Paris (13th)

1901 – (SNBA) 501 - Portrait.

83 rue de la Tombe-Issoire, Paris (14th)

1902 – (SNBA) 680 - La guitariste.

Lansdown House, Holland Park, London, G.B.

1903 – (SNBA) 751 - Domino jaune.

1904 – (SNBA) 695 - Portrait de famille.

2 Rossetti Studios, Chelsea, London, G.B.

1905 – (SNBA) 730 - Portrait de gentleman.

731 - Les trois Kimonos.

1906 – (SNBA) 720 - Portrait équestre d'un enfant.

1907 – (SNBA) 703 - Lotty and Lady.

1908 – (SNBA) 662 - Portrait (groupe).

1909 – (SNBA) 689 - Le chapeau bleu.

1910 – (SNBA) 736 - Mme la baronne de N... et ses filles.

737 - M. le baron de N...

738 - Head of a Scotsman.

1911 – (SNBA) 789 - Jour de fête en Essex.

1912 – (SNBA) 779 - Souvenirs de Noël.

1914 – (SNBA) 668 - Miss Olav Cunninghame Graham.

2 Glebe Place, Chelsea, London, G.B.

1921 – (SNBA) 659 - L'actrice.

LANE Lillias Cole

Born 20 September 1895 Waimate, NZ, died 2 October 1985 Blenheim, NZ.

Paris American Art. Co, 125 boulevard Montparnasse, Paris (6th)

1930 – (AUTOMNE) 1230 - Towers, San Gimignano.

LEIST Fredrick William

Born 21 August 1873 Sydney, NSW, died 20 March 1945 Mosman, NSW.

237 King's Road, London G.B.

1912 – (SAF) 1108 - Le miroir.

1913 – (SAF) 1091 - L'étang.

LEVER Hayley Richard

Born 28 September 1876 Bowden, South Australia, died 6 December 1958 New York, USA.

14 Carrack Dhu, Saint Ives, Cornwall, G.B.

1902 – (SNBA) 763 - Marine.

1903 – (SNBA) 844 - Effet de neige.

1904 – (SNBA) 795 - Hiver.
796 - Après-midi d'été.
797 - Les bateaux blancs.

1905 – (SNBA) 812 – 'Breezy Day', Saint Ives Harbor.
813 - Réflection Phillack.

1906 – (SNBA) 786 - Hiver.
787 - Coucher de soleil (Saint Ives).

1907 – (SNBA) 778 - Le port Saint Ives.

1908 – (SNBA) 733 - Saison de la pêche, port de Saint Ives.

1908 – (AUTOMNE) 1231 – Crépuscule, port de Saint Ives.

Saint Ives, Cornwall, G.B.

1909 – (SNBA) 601 -A haven beneath the hill Saint Ives.

LEWIS Martin

Born 7 June1881 Castlemaine, Victoria; died 22 February 1962 New York USA.

1928 – (GRAVURE MODERNE AMERICAINE)
186 - Heavy rain, gravure.
187 - Bridge near Nikko, gravure.
188 - Fishing boats in rain, gravure.

LLOYD Norman

Born 16 October 1895 Newcastle, NSW, died 5 March 1983 Yorkshire, G.B.

2 rue Bonaparte, Paris (6th)

1927 – (SAF) 1224 - Paysage, Australie.

5 rue de la Mairie, Puteaux, Seine, France.

1928 – (SAF) 1301 - Barrington Tops, Australia.
1302 - Middle Harbour, Sydney.

1929 – (SAF) 1457 - La moisson (Australia).
1458 - Après-midi (Australia).

LONGSTAFF John Campbell

Born 10 March 1861 Clunes, Victoria, died 1 October 1941 Clunes, Victoria.

Elève de M. Cormon. 15 rue Boissonade, Paris (14th)

1889 – (SAF) 1526 - Portrait de Mme L...

15 rue Boissonade, Paris (14th)

1890 – (SAF) 1534 - Portrait de Mme L...

Elève de M. Cormon. 11 rue Constance, Paris (18th)

1891 – (SAF) 1072 - Jeune mère. (mention honorable)

1892 – (SAF) 1102 - Les sirènes.

Elève de M. Cormon. 2 rue d'Odessa, Paris (14th)

1893 – (SAF) 1147 - Portrait de Mme D...

Elève de M. Cormon. 9 rue des Fourneaux, Paris (15th)

1894 – (SAF) 1192 - Portrait de Mlle M...
1193 - Portrait de M. J...

Elève de M. Cormon. 1 Carlton Hill, London G.B.

1906 – (SAF) 1062 - Portrait.

1910 – (SAF) 1227- Portrait de Mme Purcell Fitz-Gérald et de ses fils Edward et Gérald.

M

McCUBBIN Frederick
Born 25 February 1855 Melbourne, Victoria, died 20 December 1917 Melbourne, Victoria.

23 rue Delambre, Paris (14th)

1896 – (SAF) 532 - Une idylle australienne.

MacDONALD Amélia Jessie
Born near Melbourne, Victoria.

9 rue Campagne-Première, Paris (14th)

1906 – (AUTOMNE) 1085 - Boulevard Raspail.
1086 - Parc Monceau.

McELDOWNEY Iva Helen Latitia
Born 1891 Wellington, NZ.

1 Queen Victoria Street, Bank of New Zealand, London G.B.

1927 – (SAF) 1243 - Au bord de la Seine, Caudebec (Normandy).

McFURSON (sic) or MacPHERSON Fannie Fetherstonhaugh, a.k.a Fanny Holdroyd
Born 17 November 1863 Moonee Ponds, Victoria, died 1924 London

79 rue Notre-Dame-des-Champs, Paris (6th)

1890 – (SNBA) 596 - Portrait de Mlle O...

MacGAW John Thoburn
Born 1872 Hay, New South Wales, died 1952 Australia.

Saint Leonard's Forest, Horsham, Sussex, G.B.

1933 –(SAF) 1635 - Ruines du Château de Croft.
1636 - Baye de Saint Ives.

MACKENNAL Sir Edgar Bertram
Born 12 June 1863 Fitzroy, Victoria, died 10 October 1931 at Torguay, Devon G.B.

9 rue des Fourneaux, Paris

1892 – (SAF) 2839 - Tête de sainte; - relief, marble.
2840 - Baiser d'une mère; - relief, plaster.

1893 – (SAF) 3125 - Circé; - statue, plaster.
[mention honorable]

87 Clifton Hill, Saint Johns Wood, London G.B.

1894 – (SAF) 3335 - Portrait de Mme Sarah Bernhardt; - bas-relief.
3336 - Silence; bas-relief.

38 Marlborough Hill, St Johns Wood, London G.B.

1905 – (SAF) 3377 - La danseuse ; - bronze statue.
3378 - Douleur (marble statue)

1906 – (SAF) 3315 – War; - bust in bronze.

1907 – (SAF) 3097 - La Vierge et l'Enfant-Jésus; - group bronze.

MACKY Eric Spencer

Born 16 November 1880 Auckland, New Zealand, died 1958 Oakland, California.

Elève de M. J.-P. Laurens. 13 rue de l'Abbé-Grégoire, Paris (6th)

1909 – (SAF) 1186 - Le vétéran.

MacPHERSON Margaret Rose or **PRESTON** Margaret

Born 29 April 1875 Adelaide, South Australia, died 29 May 1963 Mosman, NSW.

2 rue Bréa, chez M. Lefebvre-Foinet, Paris (6th)

1905 – (SNBA) 848 - Nature morte (oignons).

1906 – (SNBA) 820 - Le chiffonnier.
821 - Nature morte (fleurs).

64 rue Madame, Paris (6th)

1913 – (SNBA) 833 - Novembre sur le balcon (nature morte).

5 Trebovir Road, Earls Court, London G.B.

1914 – (SNBA) 811 - La cuisine (nature morte).

MAISTRE Roy de

Born 27 March 1894 Bowral, NSW, died 1 March 1968 London G.B.

5 rue Léopold-Robert, Paris (14th)

1924 – (SNBA) 794 - Nature morte.

MARTIN Maximilien, or Max

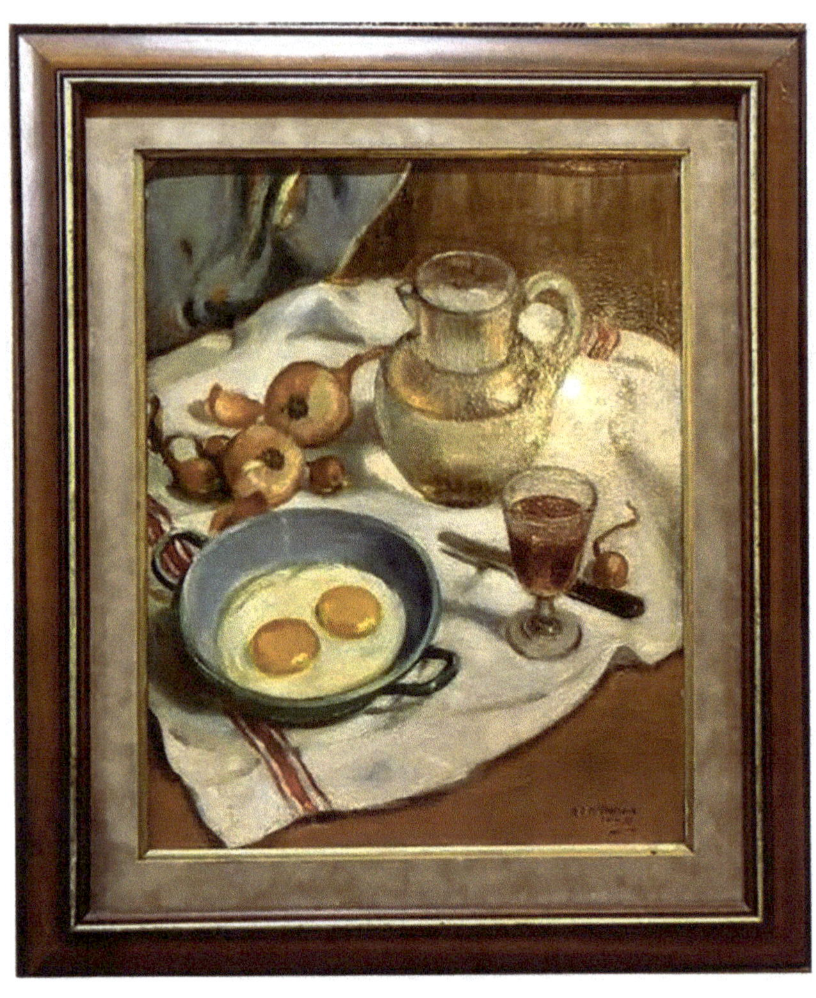

La Cuisine (*nature morte*) aka *The Kitchen*
Oil on canvas, 55 x 43 cm
Signed and dated lower right, 'M. R. McPherson/Paris 1913'
Painted in Paris, des Beaux-Arts Salon stamp to reverse.
Private Collection.

Born on 10 April 1889 Melbourne, Victoria, died in 1965 Melbourne, Victoria.

18 Fitzroy St. London, G.B.

1924 – (AUTOMNE) 1254 - Lamentation Irlandaise (peinture).

Portdown Road, Maida Vale, London, G.B.

1929 – (SAF) 1557 - Sorcellerie irlandaise.

MEESON Dora

Born 7 August 1869 Melbourne, Victoria, died 24 March 1955 Chelsea, G.B.

Elève de MM. Benjamin-Constant et J.-P. Laurens. 3 rue de Chateaubriand, Paris (8th)

1899 – (SAF) 1375 - Portrait de Mlle M...

9 Trafalgar Studios, Chelsea, London, G.B.

1908 – (SAF) 1258 - Attendant la haute marée.

Elève de Benjamin-Constant et de M. J.-P. Laurens, 1 Cedar Studios, Glebe Place, Chelsea, G.B.

1910 – (SAF) 1333 - Un jour d'été.

Elève de Benjamin-Constant et de M. Jean-Paul Laurens. 52 Glebe Place, Chelsea, London, G.B.

1911 – (SAF) 1304 - Brouillard et fumée sur la Tamise en hiver.

5191 - Les douze mois de l'année ; - esquisse d'une décoration de cheminée.

1912 – (SAF) 1290 – ' Cache-cache'.

5307 - Partie d'une frise.

1913 – (SAF) 5410 – Printemps (panneau décoratif).

1923 – (SAF) 1179 - Le pont de Londres (mention honorable).

1924 – (SAF) 1357 - Après-midi pluvieux dans le port de Londres.

1926 – (SAF) 1355 - Adélaide House, Londres en train de se construire.

1928 – (SAF) 1417 - Au-dessous du Pont de Londres.

1929 – (SAF) 1598 - Villefranche-sur-Mer.
1930 – (SAF) 1477 - La barque du Roi au pont de Londres, août 1919.
1931 – (SAF) 1571 - Villefranche-sur-Mer.
1933 – (SAF) 1745 - Appledore : North Devon.

17-18, Nassau Street, chez Bourlet and Sons Ltd., London, G.B.

1934 – (SAF) 1693 - Les bateaux pêcheurs de Hastings.
1936 – (SAF) 1686 - Le Strand, Londres sous la neige.
4099 - Westminster Hall – gravure sur cuivre.
1938 – (SAF) 1086 - Un coucher de soleil sur la Tamise.

52 Glebe Place, Chelsea, London, G.B.

1939 – (SAF) 1996 - La Rochelle.

MELDRUM Max Duncan
Born 1 December 1875 Edinburgh, Scotland , died 6 June 1955 Melbourne, Victoria.

Elève de M. J.-P. Laurens. 1 rue de l'Horloge, chez M. Nitsch, Rennes, Ille-et-Vilaine, France.

1904 – (SAF) 1255 - La leçon.

4 rue Jacob, Paris (6th)

1905 – (SAF) 1316 - Le contre-fa.

Au château de Pacé, près Rennes, Ille-et-Vilaine, France.

1908 – (SAF) 1260 - Paysan de Pacé.
1909 – (SAF) 1270 - Portrait de Mlle Yvonne Dubel, de l'Opéra.
1911 – (SAF) 1306 – 'L'homme qui rit'.

Melbourne, Australia.

1920 – (SNBA) 742 - Polonaise.

Bures, Seine-et-Oise, France.

1927 – (SNBA) 811 - Portrait (souvenir de 1912).
812 - Portrait.
813 - Portrait d'une vielle dame.
814 - Nature morte.

815 - Paysage d'Australie (temps orageux).

Gometz-le-Châtel, Seine-et-Oise, France.

1928 – (SNBA) 1323 - Chinoiseries.

Service des accrédités, Crédit-Lyonnais, Paris.

1929 – (SNBA) 1236 - Nancy Bottomley.

1237 - Portrait.

2 passage de Dantzig, Paris (15th)

1930 – (SNBA) 1314 - L'Essayage.

1315 - Le Kimono.

1316 - Nature morte.

1317 - Nature morte (Chrysanthèmes).

1318 - Portrait de l'artiste.

1931 – (SNBA) 1479 - Portrait (Alfred Boucher).

1480 - Intérieur.

The Paris American Art Co., 125 boulevard du Montparnasse, Paris (6th)

1932 – (SNBA) 1430 - Dans l'atelier.

MENPES Mortimer

Born 22 February 1855 Port Adelaide, South Australia, died 1 April 1938 Pangbourne, G.B.

Elève de R. A. Poynter. A Pont-Aven, France.

1882 – (SAF) 5484 - Maude, etching.

5485 - Three etchings.

1883 – (SAF) 4814 - Gravure.

4815 - Ditto.

Elève de M. E.-J. Poynter. Chez M. Foinet, 54 rue Notre-Dame-des-Champs, Paris (6th)

1888 – (SAF) 5375 - Pour un Un voyage au Japon, etching.

5376 - Ditto.

Elève de M. Whistler. Chez M. Patmore, 21 rue du Terrage, Paris.

1889 – (SAF) 5652 - Repas des archers, d'après FR Hals – pointe sèche.

1889 - (E.U.) — 439 - Banquet d'officiers des archers de Saint-Adrien, d'après le tableau de FR Hals, dry point.

London, G.B.

1890 – (SAF) — 5157 - Le modèle de Rembrandt, d'après Rembrandt, dry point.

1896 – (REIMS) — 1391 - Affiche: *India Paintings Drawings Etchings.* Hansard Publishing Union Limited, London. Affiche en trois couleurs : vert clair, foncé et rouge, 77 x 51. Le mot India en épargne blanche sur le rouge.

1392 - Affiche: *Paintings of France Spain and Morocco by...* S. n. imp. (London). Affiche en deux couleurs, lettres vert foncé sur vert pâle, 75 x 51.

1393 - Affich : *Paintings and drawings of Venice by...* S. n. imp. (London). Affiche en deux couleurs, brique et jaune, lettres blanches en épargne, 77 x 51.

25 Cadogan Gardens, London, G.B.

1900 – (E.U.) — 28 - Sir Henry Irving, dry point.

1900 – (E.U.) — 173 - Le XVIIIe siècle.

174 - Le parfum de la nuit, aquarelle.

MERCER Marie Cockburn

Born 19 April 1882 Roxburgh, Scotland, G.B., died 14 August 1963 at Aubaugne, France.

235 rue du Faubourg-Saint-Honoré, Paris (8th)

1913 – (AUTOMNE) — 1482 - Quartier de femmes juives (Tanger).

Jersey, G.B.

1913 – (SAF) — 1249 - Bateaux sur la plage - Valence.

1250 - Sur la plage - Valence.

MERTON Owen

Born 14 May 1887 Christchurch, NZ, died 18 January 1931 London, G.B.

59 rue Bonaparte, Paris (5th)

1913 – (INDEPENDANTS) 2078 - The lotus eaters, aquarelle.
2079 - Pont Neuf et Louvre, Paris.
2080 - Moulin à vent.

12 Castlebar Road, Ealing, London W., chez Mme Pearce.

1914 – (INDEPENDANTS) 2277 - Picolla Piazza (Ravello), aquarelle et crayon.

MONIER-WILLIAMS Cicely Hilda (nee Farmer, a.k.a. Mrs H. Warington Baden-Powell)

Born 1871 Auckland, NZ, died 7 May 1954 Scotland.

Château de Collioure, Collioure, Pyrénées-Orientales, France.

1935 – (AUTOMNE) 1120 - Nuage sur la montagne, design.

Salon d'Hiver. Grand Palais. 31ème exposition du 15 février au 15 mars 1936. Section étrangère – aquarelle-design-(pastel). Anglaise. Château de Collioure, à Collioure (P.-O.).

1936 – (HIVER) 1329 - Hiver.

Elève de M. A. Hanicotte. Château de Collioure, à Collioure (P.-O.).

1936 – (UNION DES FEMMES PEINTRES)
605 - Automne: Collioure, aquarelle.
606 - Petit port, aquarelle.

1936 – (SNBA) 1375 - Printemps. Fort Saint-Elme, design.
1376 - Hiver. Pyrénées-Orientales, design.
1377 - Eglise et tour d'horloge. Collioure, design.
1378 - Paysage de neige, design.

Salon d'Hiver. Pavillon des Salons, Esplanade des Invalides. 32ème exposition du 31 July to 5 September 1937. Section étrangere – Aquarelle-design-(pastel). Anglaise. Château de Collioure, à Collioure (P.-O.).

1937 – (HIVER) 1252 - Printemps, fort Saint-Elme (Pyr.-Or.), aquarelle.

1937 : Elève de M. A. Hanicotte. Château de Collioure, à Collioure (P.-O.).

1937 – (UNION DES FEMMES PEINTRES)

392 - Paysage en neige.
393 - Nuage sur les montagnes.

1938 – (SNBA)

871 - Mer agitée (illustration).
872 - Soir dans la montagne.
873 - Paysage Roussillonnais.
874 - Fleurs.
875 - Un coin du cellier.

1938 : Collioure (Pyrénées-Orientales), Château de Collioure.

1938 – (UNION DES FEMMES PEINTRES)

271 - Le Jiquier.

1939 – (SNBA)

879 - Dahlia.
880 - Amandier en fleurs.
881 - Roses.
882 - La Tour 'La Massane', Pyrénées-Orientales.
883 - Le Soir. Pyrénées-Orientales.
884 - Croquis de Pyrénées-Orientales.

MONTEFIORE Edward Levy

Born 1820 Barbados, died 21 October1894 Sydney, NSW.

Elève de M. Lalanne. Rue de Poitiers, Paris (9th)

1872 – (SAF)

2030 - Intérieur du palais de la Légion d'honneur, après l'incendie (mai 1871), etching.

1874 – (SAF)

3525 - Vue prise dans le parc de Nainville (Seine-et-Oise), etching.

Elève de M. Lalanne. Chez Mme Vve Cadart, 56 boulevard Haussmann, Paris (8th)

1876 – (SAF)

3931a - Rochers de Nainville, etching.
3931b - Pont-en-Royans (Isère), etching.
3931c - L'église Saint-Jacques, à Orléans, etching.
3931d - Gorges du Fier, etching.

3931e – Loches, etching.

Elève de M. Lalanne. 9 Rue de Poitiers, et chez Mme Vve Cadart, 56 boulevard Haussmann, Paris (8th)

1877 – (SAF)

4494a - Ferme de Canapville (Calvados), etching.
4494b - La maison du forgeron à Touques (Calvados), etching.
4494c - Portail du Creizker, à Saint-Pol-de-Léon (Finistère), etching.
4494d - Escalier en bois, à Morlaix (Finistère), etching.
4494e - A Vitré (Ille-et-Vilaine), etching.
4494f - A Quimper, etching.

59 rue de la Victoire, Paris (9th)

1878 – (SAF)

3511 - Eglise de Gonneville (Calvados ; Le quai d'Orsay ; Une ferme à Beuzeval (Calvados) ; Porte de Falaise (Calvados) ; - sépias.
3512 - Le ruisseau de Beuzeval ; Une ferme à Houlgate (Calvados) ; La tour Talbot à Falaise ; La falaise d'Houlgate ; designs à la plume.
4897 - D'après Eugène Fromentin, dont *Bergers kabyles*, pour *L'Art* (Sanchez et Seydoux 1877-74 et *L'embuscade*, pour la *Gazette des Beaux-Arts*, Sanchez et Seydoux 1878-13) – six gravures.
4898 - Etang de Ville-d'Avray.

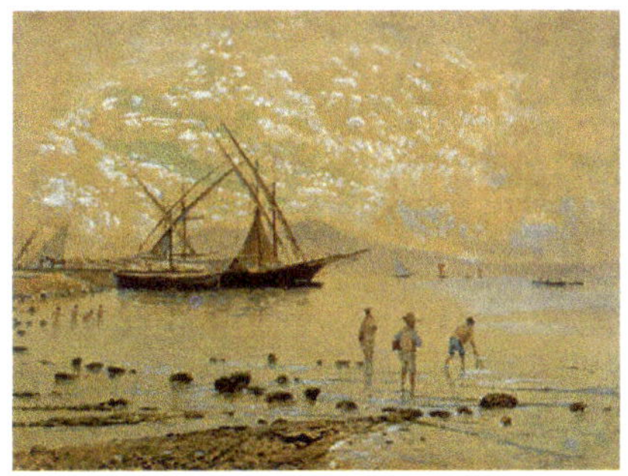

Edward Montefiore:
Bache e Pescatori a riva, 1884.

Elève de M. Lalanne. Chez Mme Vve Cadart, 56 boulevard Haussmann, Paris (8th)

1879 – (SAF)

5762-1 - Le Mesnil.
5752-2 - Allée de sycomores, au Caire.
5762-3 - Allée de parc.
5762-4 - Dannemois (Seine-et-Oise).
5762-5 - Bronze japonais.

5763 - Portrait de sir Moses Montefiore, baronnet.

1880 – (SAF) 7104 - Designs à la sépia d'après Rembrandt, two etchings.

MORRAH Elsa

Born 1900 Invercargill, NZ, died Tauranga 1989.

XXᴱ Salon: 15 may – 13 July 1930

Demeurant 12 rue des Beaux-Arts, Paris (6th)

1930 – (SOCIETE DES ARTISTES DECORATEURS)

Three decorated wooden boxes.

XXIᴱ Salon : May – July 1931

Demeurant 12 rue des Beaux-Arts, à Paris (6th)

1931 – (SOCIETE DES ARTISTES DECORATEURS)

Decorated metal boxes.

MUNTZ Margaret Joséphine or **MUNTZ-ADAMS**

Born March 30 1862 Barfold, Victoria, died November1949 Melbourne

Elève de MM. Delance, Callot et Delécluse. 37 rue d'Alésia, Paris (14th)

1892 – (SAF) 1265 - Portrait de M. le docteur Dufresne.

Elève de MM. Doucet et Bramtot. 18 rue de Milan, Paris (9th)

1893 – (SAF) 1321 - Chagrins.

MUSKETT Alice Jane

Born 28 April 1869 Fitzroy, Victoria, died 17 July 1936 Cremorne, NSW.

Elève de Mlle Hawley. 23 rue Le Vernier, Paris (17th)

1896 (SAF) 2874 – Daffodils (pastel)

Chez M. Foinet, 54 rue Notre-Dame-des-Champs, Paris (6th)

1897 (SAF) 2370 - Pastel.

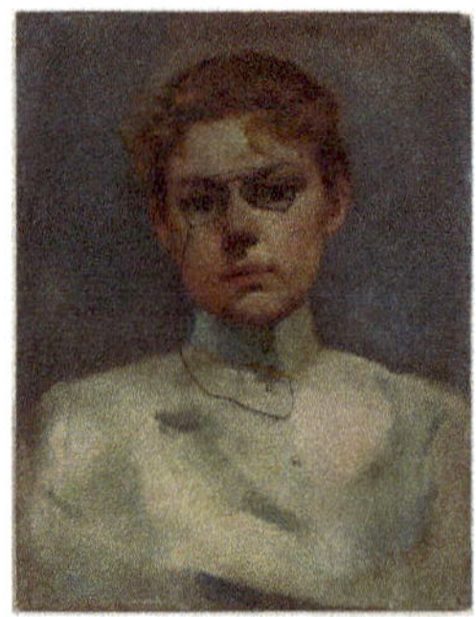

Julian Ashton: Study of Alice Muskett 1893. Oil on canvas. AGNSW.

N

NANKIVELL Frank Arthur

Born 1869 Malden, Victoria; died 1959 Morristown, USA.

1896 – (REIMS)

1248 - Poster: *The Echo.* S. n. imp. (Chicago). Datée 95. 54 x 36. Dans un paysage incolore, se détachant sous un ciel rouge, s'avance une femme vêtue de noir, s'appuyant sur une canne et semblant écouter.

1249 - Poster : *Posters in Miniature...* S. n. imp. Datée 95. Affiche en vert sur bulle, 29 x 42. Design pour une couverture ; jeune fille à cheval traversant un paysage.

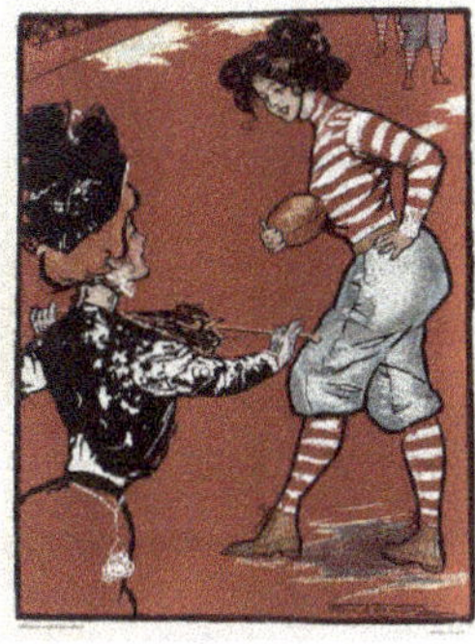

Frank Nankivell: *Progress*, 1901.

NAPIER-BELL Elise Born NZ.

51 rue d'Assas, Paris (6th)

1901 – (SNBA)

698 - La Dame en noir.

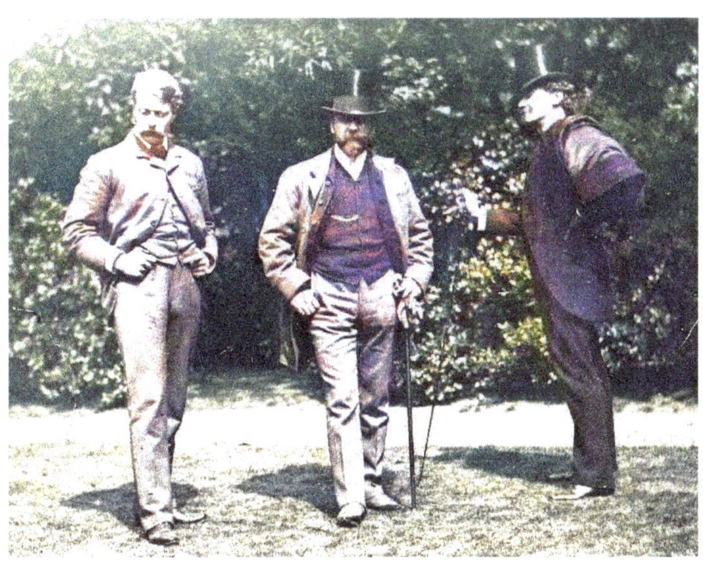

Mortimer Menpes, William M. Chase and James McNeill Whistler, Paris 1885.

O

O'CONNOR Kathleen Laetitia

Born 14 September 1876 Hokitika, NZ, died 24 August 1968 Perth, WA.

8 bis, rue Campagne-Première, Paris (14th)

1911 – (AUTOMNE) 1162 - Au jardin, painting.

1163 – Ensemble, painting.

6 passage Stanislas, Paris (6th)

1913 – (AUTOMNE) 1591 - Esquisse (Jardin du Luxembourg), painting.

1592 – Esquisse, painting.

As O'CONNOR Kathleen Gilverton (this exhibition only)

16 rue de la Grande-Chaumière, Paris (14th)

1920 – (SDAI) 3344 - Nature morte.

3345 - Portrait.

3346 - Plage de Biarritz.

3347 - Paysage.

3348 - Portrait.

3349 - Portrait.

16 rue de la Grande-Chaumière, Paris (14th)

1920 – (AUTOMNE) 1654 - Portrait au Jardin du Luxembourg.

1655 - Quatorze Juillet, design.

1656 - Nature morte, design.

52 avenue du Maine, Paris (15th)

1921 – (AUTOMNE) 1772 (p) Dans mon Atelier (Intérieur).

1773 (p) Jeu de Cartes (nature morte).

1774 (p) Bonne Chance (nature morte).

1775 (p) Nature morte.

1928 – (AUTOMNE) 1507 (p) Nature morte.

1929 – (AUTOMNE) 1123 (p) L'heure du thé.

1124 (p) La Réfugiée.

1932 – (AUTOMNE) 1301 (p) Nature morte.

Galerie Georges Petit. Société internationale des Femmes Peintres & Sculpteurs. 6 – 17 July 1934.

1934 – 176 - L'heure du thé.
177 - Red Tulips.
178 - Jardin du Luxembourg en 1913.
179 - Pauvre mère russe à Londres.

52 avenue du Maine, Paris (15th)

1935 – (UNION DES FEMMES PEINTRES)

783 - Portrait de moi-même, painting.
784 - Nature morte à la lumière bleu-gris, painting.
785 - La nourrice (Jardin du Luxembourg), painting.
786 - Nature morte, painting.
787 - Fleurs, painting.
788 - A l'Algérie, art décoratif..

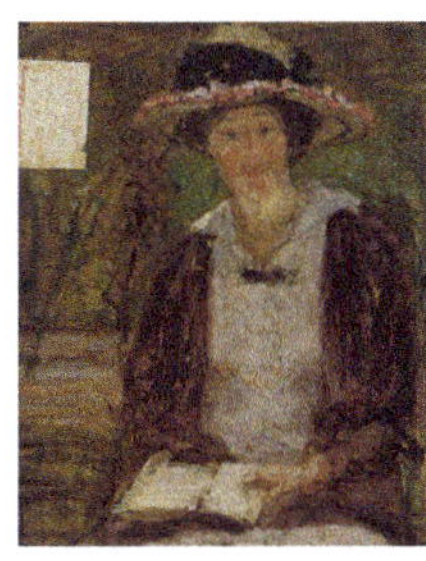

Kathleen O'Connor, *Self-portrait,* 1913.

OFFICER Edward Cairns

Born 19 September 1871 Swan Hill, Victoria, died 7 July 1921 Macedon, Victoria

Elève de MM. Benjamin-Constant et J.-P. Laurens. Etaples, Pas-de-Calais, France.

1897 – (SAF) 1275 - La nuit.
1276 - Un matin d'été à Etaples.

1898 – (SAF) 1545 - Nuages d'été.
1546 - Clair de lune.

Etaples, Pas-de-Calais, France.

1899 – (SNBA) 1116 - Au bord des sapins.
1975 - Une pastorale.
1976 - Retour des moutons.

OWEN Gladys

Born 1 July 1889 Hunters Hill, NSW, died 18 July 1960 Sydney, NSW.
Sydney, NSW, Australia.

1924 – (SNBA) 900 - La rivière.

Weekley, Kettering, G.B.

1928 – (SNBA) 1516 - Place Bab-Souira, Tunis. (d.)

P

PARKER Harold

Born 27 August 1873 Aylesbury, Buckinghamshire, G.B., died 23 April 1962 Brisbane, Queensland.

Exposition d'Art Decoratif Moderne Galerie Georges Petit, 6 - 31 December 1894 ; *Birmingham Guild of Handicraft*

1894 –

71 - D.Candélabres en cuivre jaune en fils métalliques courbés.

73 - F.Deux chandeliers en cuivre jaune

74 - G. Plaque pour porte.

77 - J. Bouton de tiroir en cuivre rouge martelé.

78 - K. Bouton de tiroir en cuivre jaune et rouge.

80 - M. Coupe en cuivre rouge martelé pour fleurs, avec anses en cuivre jaune.

82 - OP. Plaque et serrure pour porte.

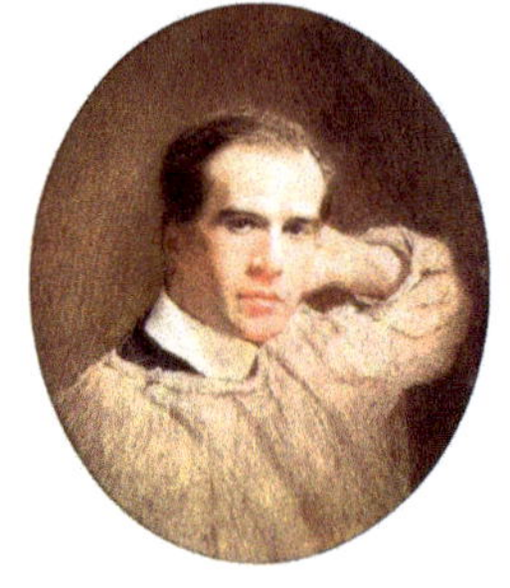

Harold Parker by Bessie Gibson.

Elève de MM. W. S. Frith et Thos. Brock. 2 Holland Lane, Kensington, London G.B.

1910 - (SAF) 3948 - Prométhée enchaîné; - statue plaster.

37 Holland Park Road, Kensington, London G.B.

1929 – (SAF) 1784 - *Horses hauling timber.*

PATTERSON Ambrose McCarthy

Born 29 June 1877 Daylesford, Victoria; died 26 December 1966 Seattle, Washington USA.

51 boulevard Saint-Jacques, Paris (14th)

1903 – (SNBA) 1015 - Nature morte.

1903 – (AUTOMNE) 433 - Par la fenêtre.

434 - Café concert.

435 - Les peupliers à Saint-Léger.

1904 – (SNBA) 981 - Fenêtre de mon atelier.
982 - Gaîté-Montparnasse.
983 - Fête

1904 – (AUTOMNE) 963 - Le mastroquet du coin.
964 - 14 juillet.
965 - Voyage du duc d'York à Melbourne.

1 rue Leclerc, Paris (14th)

1905 – (AUTOMNE) 1198 - The Green House.
1199 - The barmaid.
1200 - La plage à Sous-la-Jour.
1201 - On the beach.
1202 - Intérieur du Café.

1906 – (SDAI) 3846 - Huit études.
3847 - Steeple-chase.
3848 - Bal.
3849 - La plage, cailloux.
3850 - Vieilles maisons, à Saint-Brieuc.
3851 - Matin au bord de la mer.
3852 - Café sur la plage.
3853 - Intérieur de l'atelier.

15e expo. Société des Amis des arts de Nantes. 26 Jan - 11March 1906. Peinture. 1 rue Leclerc, Paris (14th)

1906 – (NANTES) 289 - The Green House (500 fr)
290 - Feu d'artifice (300 fr)

1906 – (SNBA) 963 - Portrait de Mlle Gudrun Hoyer Ellefsen.
964 - Coin de l'atelier.

Saint-Jean-du-Doigt, par Plougasnou, Finistère, France.

1907 – (SDAI) 3745 - Chevaux de bois.
3746 - Dorville à la Gaîté-Montparnasse.
3747 - Jeunes filles travaillant dans l'atelier.
3748 - Tolède, prise de la maison Cervantès.

3749 - Fête de nuit.
3750 - Intérieur d'auberge.

1907 – (AUTOMNE) 1377 - Le Kimono au Japon.
1378 - Paysanne au jardin.
1379 - Fleurs (Poppies and sweet peas).
1380 - Fleurs.

17e expo. Société des Amis des arts de Nantes. 31Jan – 15March 1908.
19 rue Daguerre, Paris (14th)

1908 – (NANTES) 465 - La plage de Saint-Jean-du-Doigt (400 fr)
466 - Falaises, journée grise (400 fr)

Saint-Jean-du-Doigt, par Plougasnou, Finistère, France, et 37 rue de la Charité, Bruxelles, Belgium..

1908 – (AUTOMNE) 1608 - The violet gown.
1609 - Marine argent (coucher de soleil).
1610 - Poppus.

19 rue Daguerre, Paris (14th)

1908 – (SDAI) 4620 - Nature morte.
4621 - Après le Bain.
4622 - Bébé.
4623 - Course de Taureaux.
4624 - Maison-Blanche.
4625 - Fruits et Fleurs.

PAUL Emile
Born in Australia.

Elève de M. Renard. Rue Delambre, hôtel Delambre, Paris (14th)

1910 – (SAF) 4911 - Moulin en Hollande, etching.

PAXTON Josephine
Born Sydney, NSW.

60 Gordon Mansions, Francis Street, London G.B.

1930 – (SDAI) 3299 - Une marchande de fleurs, Londres (1400 fr)
3300 - Nu (1200 fr)

1930 – (AUTOMNE) 1621 - Le dernier bouquet du soir, Londres.

48 Upper Cheyne Row, Chelsea, London G.B.

1931 – (SDAI) 3170 - Bohémienne de la New Forest (1200 fr)

3171 - L'heure du thé, Londres (1400 fr)

10 Great Saint Andrew Street, chez J. Etienne (Chenue), London G.B.

1934 – (SDAI) 3437 - Le petit bouquet.

3438 - Jeune paysan italien.

1935 – (SDAI) 2717 - L'Australienne (1100 fr)

2718 - L'amandier (550 fr)

1936 – (SDAI) 2605 - Peinture.

2606 - Peinture.

1937 – (SDAI) 2439 - Le chapeau bleu (not for sale).

2440 - Vieux paysan (500 fr)

PERRY Adelaide Elizabeth

Born 23 June 1891 Beechworth, Victoria, died 19 November 1973 Killara, NSW.

Stanley Gardens, 18 Notting Hill Gate, London G.B.

1924 – (SAF) 1530 - Portrait of the Rev. Frederick Campion.

1531 - By the window.

PHILLIPS Rosetta Phoebe

Born 1871 Melbourne, Victoria, died 1 August 1953 Hastings, East Sussex G.B.

218 boulevard Raspail, Paris (14th)

1920 – (AUTOMNE) 1745 - Château Blaraz.

PIGUENIT William Charles

Born 27 August 1836 Hobart, Tasmania, died 17 July 1914 Hunters Hill, NSW.

Hunter's Hill, N.S.Wales, Sydney, Australia.

1893 – (SAF) 1422 - Paysage.

POOL SMITH Leslie Robert

Born New Zealand.

Episy, Seine-et-Marne, France.

1921 – (AUTOMNE) 1918 (p) L'esclave.

Episy, par Moret-sur-Loing, Seine-et-Marne, France.

1926 – (SAF) 1587 - Djerba.

1588 - Les femmes du Mellah (Meknes).

1927 – (SAF) 1536 - Soleil du printemps.

1537 - Pêcheurs d'Azzemour (Maroc).

POWER Harold Septimus

Born 31 December 1877 Dunedin, NZ, died 3 January 1971 Richmond, Victoria.

11 Finch Lane, Bushey, G.B.

1932 – (SAF) 1960 - The Coster.

1961 - Polo.

Meadow Studios, 11 High Street, Bushey, Hertfordshire, G.B.

1935 – (SAF) 1857 - London Street Scene.

PRESTON Margaret, see **MacPHERSON** Margaret Rose

Q

QUINN James

Born 4 December 1869 Melbourne, Victoria, died 18 February 1951 Melbourne Victoria.

Elève de MM. J.-P. Laurens et Benjamin-Constant. 8 boulevard du Montparnasse, Paris (6th)

1895 – (SAF) 1574 - Portrait de Mlle H...

1575 - Un cavalier.

33 boulevard du Montparnasse, Paris (6th)

1897 – (SNBA) 1036 - La Nativité.

Elève de MM. Benjamin-Constant et J.-P. Laurens. 33 boulevard Edgard-Quinet, Paris (14th)

1898 – (SAF) 1668 - Chagrin.

1669 - Mère et enfants.

1899 – (SAF) 1605 - Famille de pêcheurs, à Etaples (Pas-de-Calais).

1606 - Portrait.

Etaples, chez M. Joos, Pas-de-Calais, France.

1900 – (SAF) 1089 - Paysage.

109a New Kings Road, Fulham, London G.B.

1912 – (SAF) 1540 - Mère et fils. (mention honorable)

1541 - Frères.

1913 – (SAF) 1481 - Portrait de Mlle Marguerite Lloyd.

1482 - Halles aux poissons.

1914 – (SAF) 1660 - Portrait de Harold Power.

1923 – (SAF) 1396 - La veuve.

1924 – (SAF) 1607 - Portrait of John Tweed, sculpteur.

1608 - Portrait of Lady Abdy, femme de Sir Robert Abdy.

1926 – (SAF) 1618 - Mois d'avril en Angleterre (G.B.).

1927 – (SAF) 1569 - La petite Dame en gris.

1928 – (SAF) 1650 - Portrait de Mme A. E. H. Cull.

1651 - Portrait de Mlle M. E. Brough. M. A., maîtresse d'école à Mare, Angleterre, Grande-Bretagne.

1929 - (SAF) 1887 - Violet Ann wife of T. Gilbert Scott, esq.

1888 - Portrait de Mme A. E. K. Cull.

1930 - (SAF) 1734 - Asphodèles.

1735 - René, le chercheur.

1933 - (SAF) 2092 - Her Royal Highness, the Duchess of York. (illustration)

2093 - Henry Whittaker FR S. A., President of the Blackburn Society of Antiquarians.

R

RAE Alison

Born 6 October 1858, Melbourne, Victoria, died 24 May 1945, Hastings, G.B.

1912-Douai : Sté des Amis des Arts de Douai. 7 July – 4 August 1912. Rue des Voiliers, Etaples (Pas-de-Calais).

1912 – 225 - Les Chrysanthèmes (gouache).

226 - Intérieur étaplois (gouache).

1913-Douai : Sté des Amis des Arts de Douai. 6 July – 3 August 1913.

1913 – 203 - Fleurs et Nature Morte (Gouache).

204 - Le Bouquet (Gouache).

1914-Douai : Sté des Amis des Arts de Douai. 12 July – 2 August1914.

1914 – 287 - Pensées (gouache).

288 - Pensées (gouache).

R

RAE Isobel or "Iso"
Born 18 August 1860 Melbourne, Victoria, died 16 March 1940 Brighton, G.B.

Holland Park Road, London, G.B.

1889 – (E.U.) 131 - Eurydice. (mention honorable)

27 avenue Carnot, Paris (17th)

1890 – (SNBA) 719 - Portrait de Mlle R…
1891 – (SNBA) 750 - Tête de garçon.

32e Exposition municipale des beaux-arts à Rouen. 1 Oct.-30 Nov. 1891. Elève de MM. Courtois et Rixens. 27 Avenue Carnot, Paris (17th)

1891 – (ROUEN) 701 - Intérieur en Picardie.
702 - Un petit paysan.

13 rue Le Verrier, Paris (6th)

1892 – (SNBA) 823 - Dans les bois.
1893 – (SNBA) 855 - Au soleil.

1893 Dunkerque : Société Dunkerquoise. Supplement. Peinture. Etaples, France.

1893 724 - Un appel.

Etaples, Pas-de-Calais, France.

1894 – (SNBA) 939 - Echappée.
940 - Flirt.
1895 – (SNBA) 1031 - La solitude.
1896 – (SNBA) 1039 - Le travail.
1897 – (SNBA) 1040 - Le soir.

Ackland Road, Upper Norwood, London, G.B.
Avesnes : IIe Exposition Artistique. Peinture. Salle III – Région d'Avesnes. Voituron (Mlle Jeanne). Grand'Place, Avesnes, France.

1897 – 113 - Le bébé rose, copie d'après Iso Ray - tableau.
1900 – (E.U.) 213 - La cigale.

Rue des Voiliers, Etaples, Pas-de-Calais, France.

1908 – (SNBA) 1645 - Matelots du Trépor.

Douai : 54e exp. Sté Amis des Arts de Douai. 12 juil.- 9 août 1908.
Elève de Courtois. Rue des Voiliers, Etaples (Pas-de-Calais).

1908 – 174 - Ramasseuses de Fagots. (300 fr.)
175 - Effet du soir à Etaples. (250 fr.)

1909 – *Elève de Courtois. 55e Exposition. Société des Amis des Arts de Douai. Catalogue des tableaux & Œuvres d'Art.*

221 - Peinture à l'huile (650 fr)
222 - Une tricoteuse (150 fr.)

19e expo. Société des Amis des arts de Nantes. 20 Feb – 3 April 1910.

1910 – (NANTES) 432 - Jeune Mère (1250 fr)

1910 – (SNBA) 1034 - Le baisier.
1035 - L'adoré.

Elève de Courtois. Rue des Voiliers, à Etaples, Pas-de-Calais, France.
56e Exposition. Société des Amis des Arts de Douai. Catalogue des tableaux & Œuvres d'Art.

1910 – 149 - Journée chaude (800 fr)
150 - A l'ombre (800 fr)

1911 – (SNBA) 1087 - Portrait de Mlle R…

Elève de M. Courtois. Rue des Voiliers, Etaples, Pas-de-Calais, France.
57e Exposition. Société des Amis des Arts de Douai. Catalogue des tableaux & Œuvres d'Art.

1911 – 199 - L'heure de la Marée.
200 - Les Baigneurs.

1912 – 1079 - Simone et la bonne.

1912-Douai : Sté des Amis des Arts de Douai. 7 July - 4 August 1912.
Elève de Courtois. Rue des Voiliers, Etaples (Pas-de-Calais).

1912 – (SNBA) 227 – Thérèse endimanchée.
228 – A la Plage.

1913 – (SNBA) 1030 - Les acheteuses.

1913-Douai : Sté des Amis des Arts de Douai. 6 July - 3 August 1913.
Elève de M. Gustave Courtois. Rue des Voiliers, Etaples (Pas-de-Calais).

1913 – 205 - La Petite Sœur (fusain et pastel).
206 - La Petite Rousse et son Frère

1914 – (SNBA) 981 - L'attente.

1914-Douai : Sté des Amis des Arts de Douai. 12 July - 2 August 1914. Elève de M. Gustave Courtois. 3, rue des Violiers, Etaples (Pas-de-Calais).

286 - L'Enfant.

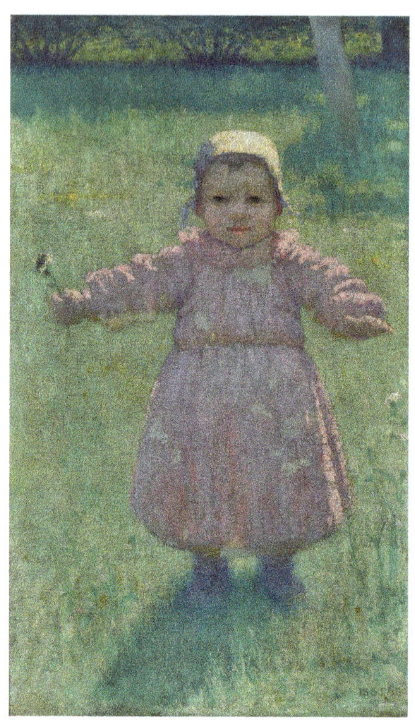

Iso Rae: *Young Girl at Etaples*, 1892.

Cher Mme Errant, à Etaples, Pas-de-Calais, France.

1921 – (SNBA) 1500 - En route pour le bal, aquarelle.

1501 - Intervalle, gouache.

1502 - L'entrée du bal, gouache.

RAMSAY Hugh

Born 25 March 1877 Glasgow, Scotland, died 5 March 1906 Clydebank, Scotland.

Elève de MM. Courtois, Girardot et Raphaël Collin, boulevard Saint-Jacques, Paris (14th)

1901 – (SAF) 1668 - Portrait de M. M.

1902 – (SNBA) 974 - Portrait de M. P.

975 - Portrait de Mlle L...

976 - Jeanne.

977 - Nature morte.

RENTOUL OUTHWAITE Ida

Born 9 June 1888 Melbourne, Victoria, died 25 June 1960 Melbourne, Victoria.

Galerie Georges Petit. Exposition Ida Rentoul Outhwaite. Designs. Elves and Fairies. 1 – 14 October 1920.

1920 – The copyrights of all pictures sold are reserved.

1 - The Glow-worm.

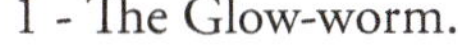

2 - The Happy Isles.

3 - The Dark Pool.

4 - The Dear Old Friend.

5 - The Doctor.

6 - The Witch Child.

7 - The Love Song.

8 - Fairy Chimes.

9 - Rivals.

10 - The Elopement.

11 - Going the Pace.

12 - The Jazz Band.

13 - I Care for Nobody.

14 - The Question.

15 - The Enchantress.

16 - The Interval.

17 - Bubbles.

18 - Broken Wings.

19 - Good Company.

20 - A Nocturne.

21 - The Solo.

22 - The Postman.

23 - Revellers.

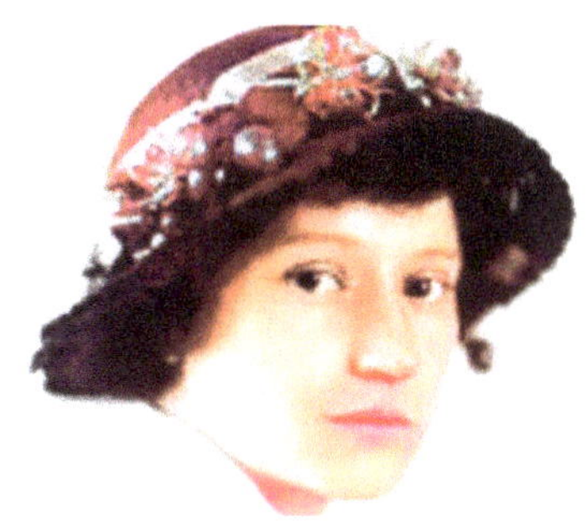

Ida Rentoul Outhwaite

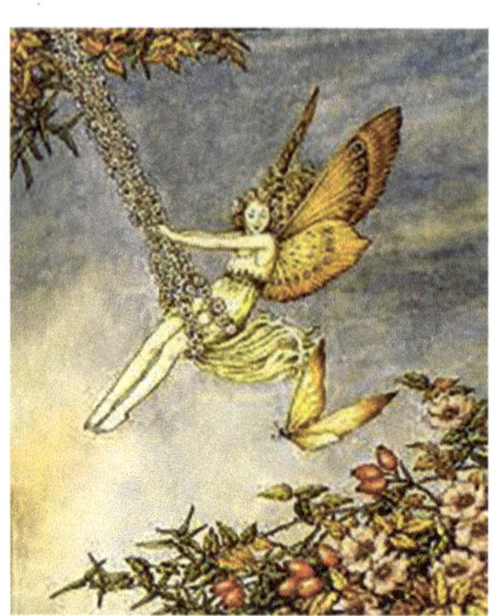

Ida Rentoul Outhwaite:
The Daisy Swing, 1920.

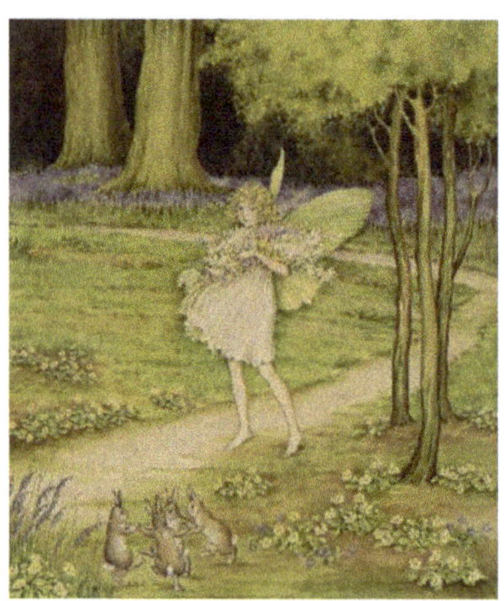

Ida Rentoul Outhwaite:
Spring, 1921.

24 - The Proposal.
25 - Feminine Fears.
26 - When we don't Believe in Fairies.
27 - The Jazz.
28 - The Calling Sea.
29 - Election Day.
30 - The Fairies are so Shy.
31 - Washing Day.
32 - Thrown Out.
33 - The Sea-Urchin.
34 - What the Moon Saw.
35 - The Ambush.
36 - Rolling the Pitch.
37 - The First Flight.
38 - Castaway.
39 - Moonrise.
40 - The Comforters.
41 - The Air Ship.
42 - The End of the Quarrel.
43 - The Gossip.
44 - The Solo.
45 - Button Day.
46 - Glow-worm Lamps.
47 - The Trysting Place.
48 - Drifting.
49 - Modes et Robes.
50 - The Swing.
51 - The First Bird Song.
52 - War.
53 - Spring on Gallipoli.
54 - Forsaken.
55 - His Audience.
56 - The Party.
57 - Snowflakes.
58 - The Kaisers Dream

REYNELL Gladys
Born 4 September 1881 Glenelg, South Australia, died 16 November 1956 Melbourne, Victoria.

64 rue Madame, Paris (6th)

1913 – (SNBA) 1060 - Enfant nu.

RIGGAL Louisa Blanche
Born 2 March 1868 Castlemaine, Victoria, died 31 august 1918, Rouen, France.

7 rue Léopold-Robert, boulevard du Montparnasse, Paris (14th)

1899 – (SNBA) 1225 - Portrait de Miss H...

RIX Hilda Emily, or **RIX NICHOLAS,** Hilda (from 1916)
Born 1 September 1884 Ballarat, Victoria, died 3 August 1961 Delegate, NSW.

Peinture. Etaples (Pas-de-Calais).

1913 – (SOCIETE DES PEINTRES ORIENTALISTES)

693 - Femme arabe.
694 - Femme masquée.
695 - Marocaine.
696 - Marchand de bonbons à Tanger, design de couleurs.
697 - Au rendez-vous, design de couleurs.
698 - Marchand de fruits, design de couleurs.
699 - Groupe d'amis, design de couleurs.
700 - Le Sokko, design de couleurs.
701 - Famille marocaine, design de couleurs.
702 - Les mains de la Fathma, design de couleurs.
703 - Marchand d'oranges, design de couleurs.
704 - Marchands de pain, design de couleurs.
705 - Le grand Sokko à Tanger, design de couleurs.
706 - Porte à Tanger, design de couleurs.

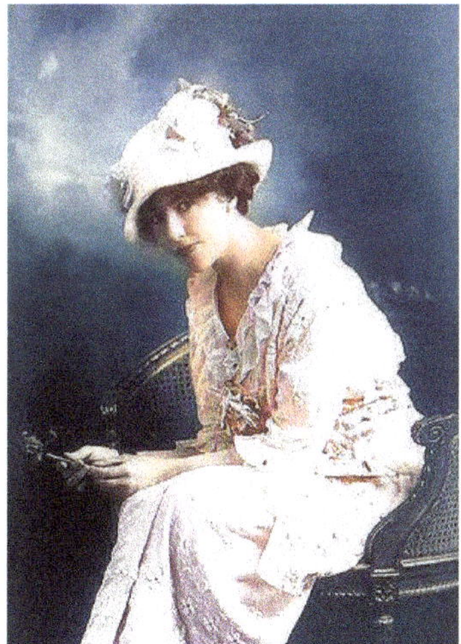

Hilda Rix Nicholas.

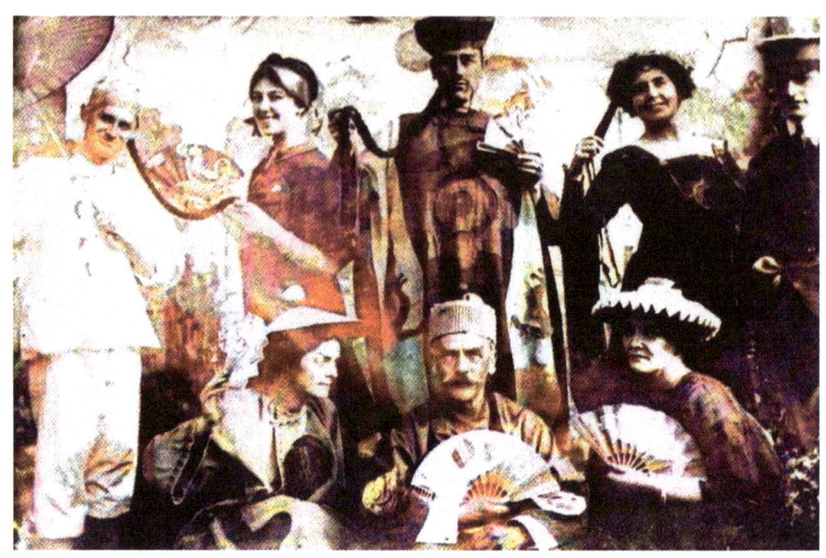

Painters at Etaples: (left to right, standing) C.A. Slade, Hilda Rix, Arthur Baker Clack, Elsie Rix, F. Potter; (sitting) unknown, M. Gwilt-Jolley, Edith Baker Clack, c1913.

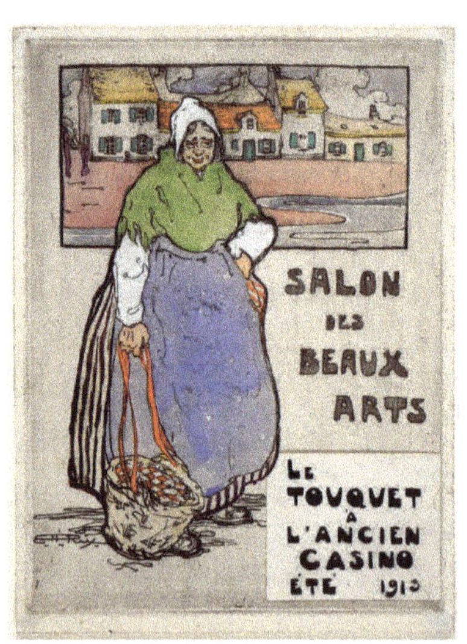

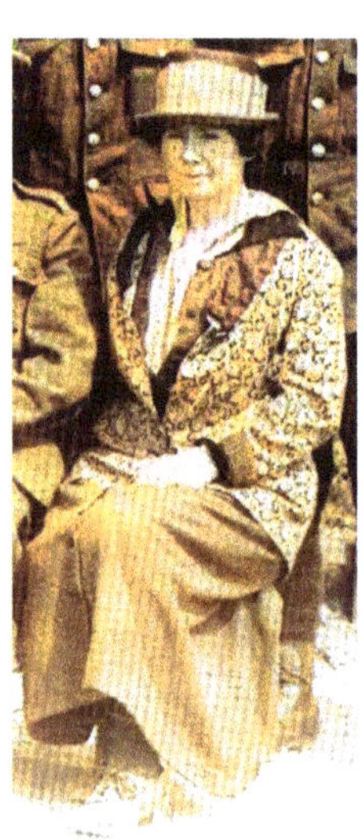

(Left): Poster for the 1913 Salon des Beaux-Arts by Hilda Rix (Nicholas); (Right) Isobel Rae at Etaples, c1918.

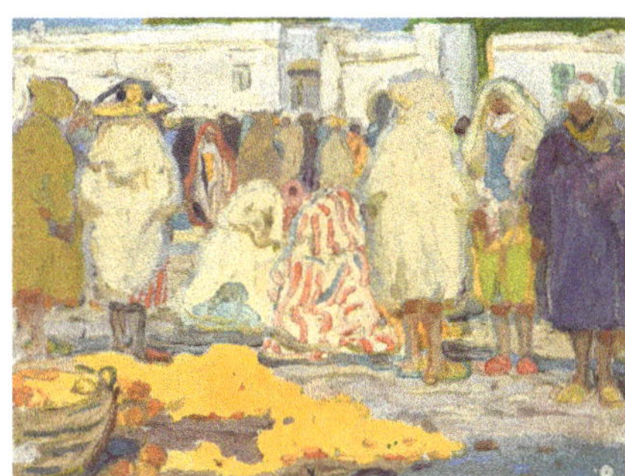

Hilda Rix: *Morrocan market,* 1913.

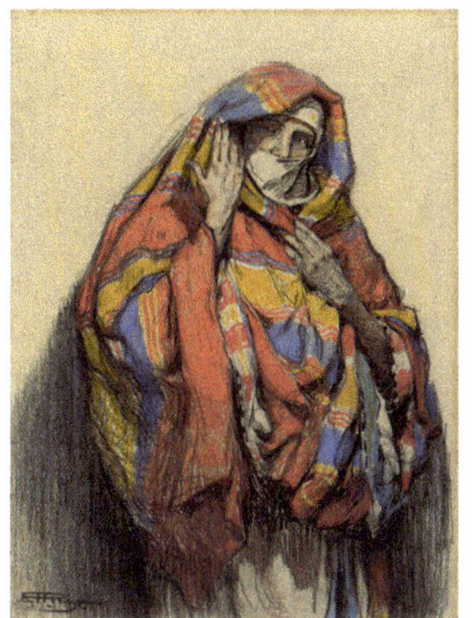

Hilda Rix: *Camoflauge,* 1913.

707 - Arabes, design de couleurs.
708 - Femmes Arabes,
design de couleurs.
709 - Près de la porte du Sokko,
design de couleurs.
710 - Discussion, design de couleurs.
711 - Jeune Riffain, design de couleurs.
712 - Jeune esclave marocaine,
design de couleurs.
713 - Sur la pente du Sokko,
design de couleurs.
714 - Boutiques sur le marché,
design de couleurs.
715 - Un restaurant, design de couleurs.
716 - Selles rouges marocaines,
design de couleurs.
717 - Marchands de charbon de bois,
design de couleurs.
718 - Marchands de sel,
design de couleurs.
719 - Conversation, design de couleurs.
720 - La porte orange,
design de couleurs.
721 - Jeune Marocain,
design de couleurs.

Chez M. Manzotti, 113 rue Notre-Dame-des-Champs, Paris (6th)
1913 : Exposition universelle et internationale de Gand. Œuvres exécutées au Maroc par les Membres de la Société des Peintres Orientalistes Français.

1913 – (SOCIETE DES PEINTRES ORIENTALISTES)

150 - Musicienne marocaine, painting.
151 - Femme de Tanger, painting.
152 - Ecrivain public à Tanger
(Design de couleurs).

153 - Dans la rue. Tanger
(Design de couleurs).
154 - Marchand de citrons, Tanger
(Design de couleurs).
155 - Boutiques à Tanger
(Design de couleurs).

1914 : Peinture. Miss Hilda Rix. Etables, Pas-de-Calais, France..

1914 – (SOCIETE DES PEINTRES ORIENTALISTES)

702 - La Robe chinoise.
703 - Une Danseuse espagnole.
704 - Dans le jardin d'un café espagnol.
705 - Souvenir de Chine.
706 - Dans le Soleil d'Espagne.
707 - La Soledad, design.
708 - Danse d'Espagne, design.
709 - Une Femme du Maroc, design.
710 - A Tetuan, design.
711 - Dans un café arabe, design.
712 - Une Fille du peuple
d'Espagne, design

Galerie Georges Petit. Exposition de Tableaux d'Australie par Mme Hilda Rix Nicholas. 16 – 30 January1925.

1925 – PAINTINGS

1 - Magie d'automne.
2 - Le Ruisseau argenté.
3 - Son pays.
4 - La Barrière verte.
5 - Mon jardin à l'automne ; Sydney.
6 - La Baie de Mosman ; Sydney.
7 - Jeune Fille de la brousse.
8 - Eucalyptus blanc.
9 - Mon jardin au printemps.
10 - Tondeurs de moutons.
11 - Cimes empourprées.
12 - L'Eucalyptus bronzé.

13 - La Vallée au printemps.
14 - Snowy River.
15 - En Australie [reproduced in catalogue, homme à cheval fumant la pipe].
16 - Nuages qui passent.
17 - Les Trois Sœurs ; montagnes bleues.
18 - L'Ecurie.
19 - La Hutte.
20 - Le Verger.
21 - Pionnière.
22 - Matin de printemps.
23 - Les Saules.
24 - A travers les eucalyptus [reproduced in catalogue].
25 - Baigneuses.
26 - Le Chant de l'oiseau.
27 - Le Joyeux Soldat.
28 - Nuages.
29 - Près de la fenêtre.
30 - Maternité [reproduced in catalogue].
31 - Nuages de pluie.
32 - Mon atelier ; Sydney.
33 - Le Guerrier.

DESIGNS

34 - Deux Soldats [reproduced in catalogue].
35 - Major G. M. Nicholas D. S. O.
36 - Saules dorés.
37 - La Hutte du chasseur.
38 - Soldat australien.
39 - L'Arbre tordu.
40 - Joie de vivre.
41 - Un Anzac.
42 - Saules verts.

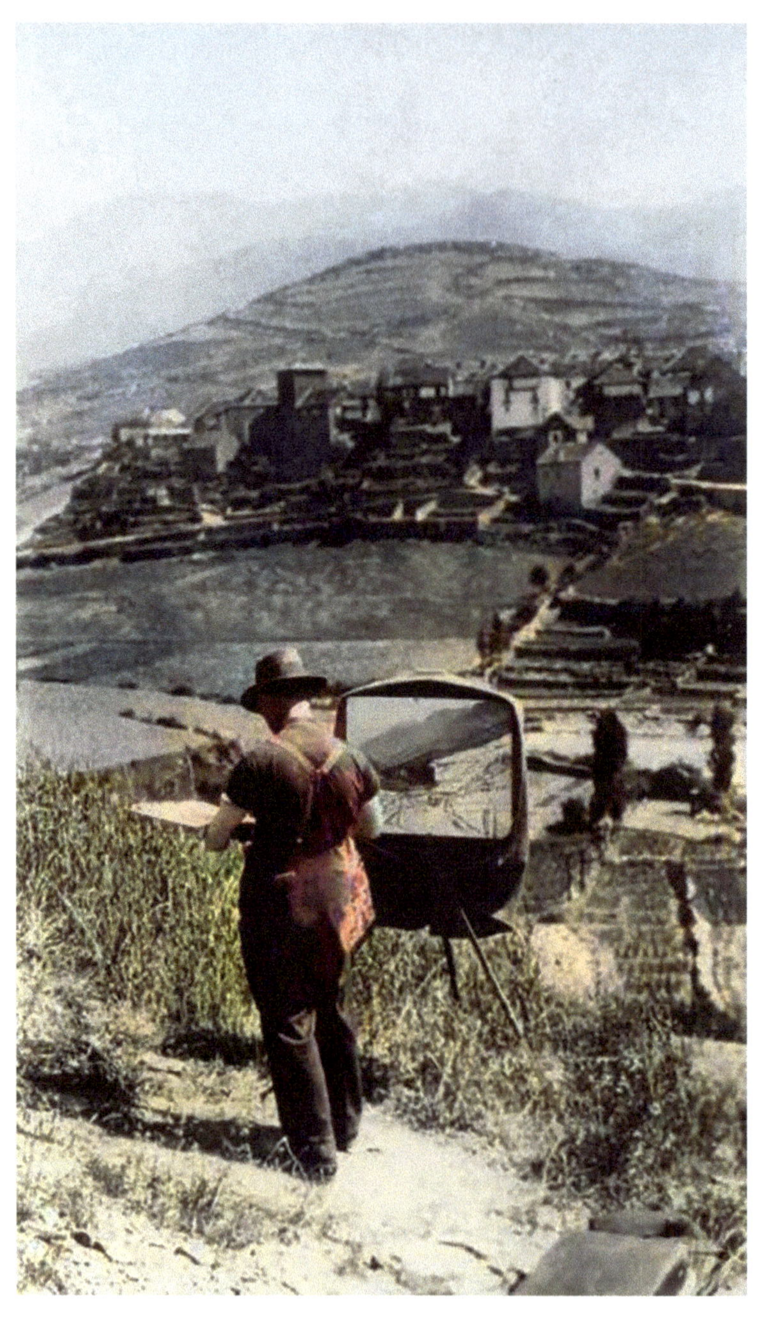

Herbert Rose painting in France 1934.

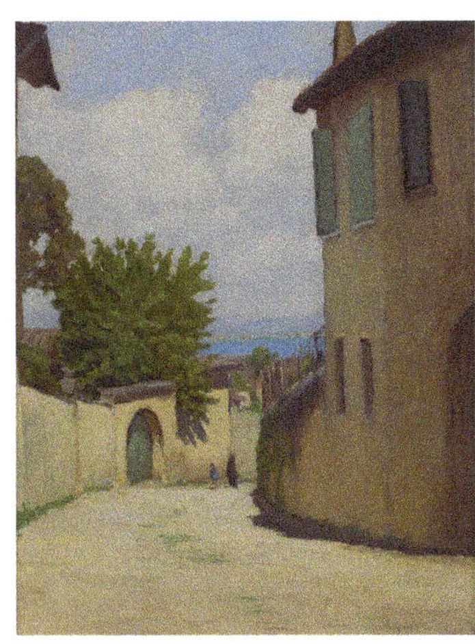

Herbert Rose:
Street, Cagnes-sur-Mer, oil on board.

43 - L'Abri.
44 - Le Seuil.
45 - Cheval de labour.
46 - Officier des boy-scouts.
47 - Songe d'enfant.
48 - Aube ; Sydney.
49 - La Scierie.
50 - Sylvia en bleu.
51 - 'June'.
52 - Gamin australien.
53 - Boy-scout.
54 - La Cabane.
55 - Famille de chiens de bergers.
56 - Lieut. B. FR Nicholas M. C.
57 - En France.

ROSE Herbert
Born 1890 Melbourne, Victoria, died January 1937 Delhi, India.
18 West Cromwell Road, London, G.B.
1936 – (SAF) 2088 - Coin du marché, Tétouan, Maroc, illustration.
2089 - Le grand canal de Venise.

ROWELL John Thomas Nightingale
Born 18 January 1894 Melbourne, Victoria, died 14 November 1973 Mornington, Victoria.
17 Nassau Street, chez Bourlet and Sons Ltd., London G.B
1938 – (SAF) 1356 - Quiet Harbour.

RUSSELL John Peter
Born 16 June 1858 Darlinghurst, NSW; died 22 April 1930 Randwick, NSW.
Goulfar, Belle-Isle-en-Mer, Morbihan, France.
1905 – (AUTOMNE) 1388 - Cruach en Mahr (matin).
Galerie Georges Petit. Société internationale d'aquarellistes. 16 – 30 November 1905.
1905 – 216 - Déclin de jour d'hiver, à Belle-Isle.
217 - Rochers, à Belle-Isle.
218 - Le Pêcheur de congres.

219 - Tempête à Belle-Isle.
En portefeuille :
220 - Vingt-deux aquarelles.

Goulfar, Belle-Isle-en-Mer, Morbihan, et villa Méquille, Neuilly-sur-Seine, Seine, France.

1906 – (SDAI) 4411 - Mer agitée.
4412 - Environ d'Antibes (matin).
4413 - Soleil et tempête.
4414 - L'aiguille (soleil d'hiver).
4415 - Jour brumeux de printemps.
4416 - Les anguilles à Belle-Isle.
4417 - Polyte pêcheur
4418 - Étude de plein air.

Galerie Georges Petit. 2ème exposition - Société internationale d'aquarellistes. 16 – 30 November 1906.

1906 – 166 - Petite vallée.
167 - Cros-Marion.
168 - Roc-Toul.
169 - Le temps se gâte.
En portefeuille :
170 - Vingt aquarelles.

1907 – (SDAI) 4332 - Roc-Ioul.
4333 - Voile rouge.
4334 – Étude
4335 - L'aiguille.
4336 - Cathédrale de Lincoln (Angleterre G.B.).

Galerie Georges Petit. 3ème exposition – Société internationale d'aquarellistes. 18 – 30 November 1907.

1907 – 213 - Marine.
214 - Marine.
215 - Marine.
216 - Marine.
En carton :
217-243 25 aquarelles.

56 rue Borghèse, Neuilly-sur-Seine, Seine, France.

1908 – (SDAI)	5333 - Pêcheur de Congres.
	5334 - Pêcheur de Congres.
	5335 - Pêcheur de Congres.
	5336 - Aquarelle.
	5337 - Aquarelle.
	5338 - Aquarelle.
1909 – (SDAI)	1399 - Untitled.
	1400 – Ditto.

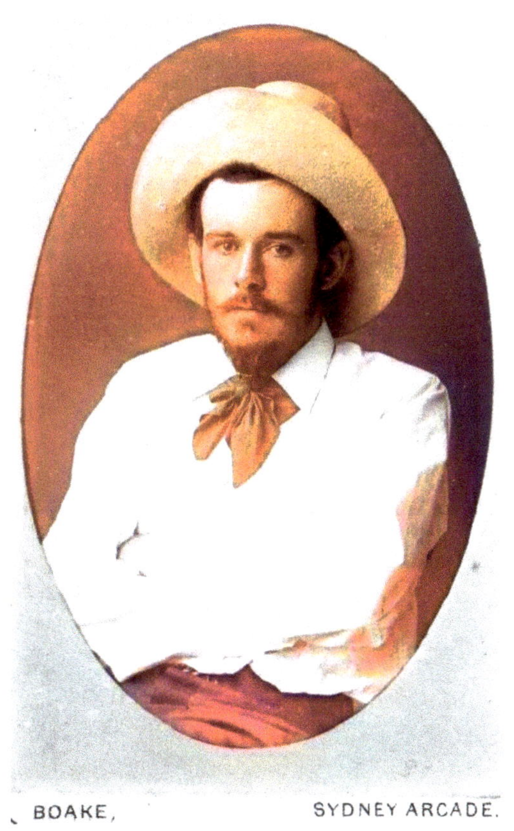

John Peter Russell in Sydney 1883, about to leave for Europe.

S

SAINT-MAUR-MORSE Marie

Born in Great Britain

1900-Roubaix-Tourcoing : 22e Exposition Sté Artistique de Roubaix-Tourcoing. 22 Sept.- 29 Oct. 1900. Elève de son père. Médaille d'argent, exposition de Bordeaux. A Chatron par Néauphle-le-Château (S.-et-O.).

1900 – 305 -Chiens.
306 - Le lac Commewarry (Australie du Sud).

Expose au Salon de Bordeaux en 1901 (voir à Saint-Maur-Morse-Ap-Ivys Mlle Marie).

SAINT-PAUL Alexander Angove

Born Adelaide, South Australia.

20 boulevard Poissonnière, Paris (9th)

1934 – (SAF) 2182 - Chrysanthèmes.

1936 – (SAF) 2125 - Portrait de Mme X...

SAINT-PAUL Alla

Born Adelaide, South Australia

20 boulevard Poissonnière, Paris (9th)

1932 – (AUTOMNE) 1516 - Anémones.

SCIZE Pierre aka Francois Michel Piot

Born 17 February 1894, Pont-de-Chéruy, France, died 10 December 1956, Melbourne, Victoria.

1926 – (LYON) Salon des écrivains (p. 26)
Le Printemps sur la tour Eiffel.

SCOTT Eric Giddon

Born 1902 Bega NSW; died 1978.

37 rue Froidevaux, Paris (14th)

1923 – (SAF) 4419 - L'hiver à Neuilly, etching.
4420 - L'hôtel de Sens, etching.

1924 – (SAF) 4661 - Rue des deux Ponts.
4662 - Vue du Pont National.

1926 – (SAF) 4312 - Vieux Chartres, etching.
4313 - Somme à Amiens, etching.
1927 - (SAF) 4190 - Chapelle à Vence, etching.
4191 - Printemps le midi, etching.
1928 – (SAF) 4306 - San-Georgia. Venise, etching.
4307 - Grand Canal. Venise, etching.
1929 – (SAF) 4596 - Le broc, etching.
4597 - Village de pêcheurs, etching.

SCOTT James Fraser
Born 24 September 1877, Dunedin NZ, died 25 April 1932 London, G.B.

Elève de MM. Benjamin-Constant et Jean-Paul Laurens. 77 Amalier Strasse, Munich, Germany.

1901 – (SAF) 1823 - Intérieur hollandais.

Saint Oswald's Studios, 5 Sedlescombe Road, London, G.B.

1928 – (SAF) 1798 - Portrait of A. W. Goodman, Barrister, London.

SHERWOOD Maud Winifred Kimbell
Born 22 December 1880 Dunedin, NZ ; died 1 December 1956 Katoomba, NSW.

Chez Thos. Cook et Sons, Nice, Alpes-Maritimes, France.

1927 – (SDAI) 3390 - Bateaux vénitiens, aquarelle.
1928 – (SDAI) 3957 - Château Doria, aquarelle (4000 fr)

SHORE Arnold Joseph
Born 5 May 1897 Melbourne, Victoria, died 22 May 1963 Melbourne, Victoria.

66 Union Street, Windsor, Melbourne (Australia)

1930 – (AUTOMNE) 1860 – Ranunculus, painting.

SIMON Naomi B.
Born Sydney, NSW.

29 Arundel Gardens, London, G.B.

1931 – (SAF) 2037 - The Artist's studio.
1939 – (SAF) 2533 bis - Three roses.

SMYTHE Marjorie Kane
Born Sydney, NSW.

9 rue de la Grande-Chaumière, Paris (6th)

1925 – (AUTOMNE) 1248 - Le jardin du Luxembourg.

STEPHENS Ethel Anna or Anne aka Mrs David Fox

Born 1864 Sydney, NSW, died 1940 Australia.

65 boulevard Arago, Paris (13th)

1921 – (SNBA) 1042 - Nature morte.

1922 – (SNBA) 897 - La fontaine du Château.

STREETON Arthur

1867 Melbourne, Australia … 1943 Melbourne

Chez M. Conder, 13 rue Ravignan, Paris (18th)

1892 – (SAF) 1560 - Golden summer. (Mention honorable)

Chez MM. Paul Foinet fils et Lefebvre, 54 rue Notre-Dame-des-Champs, Paris (6th)

1902 – (SAF) 1527 - Gelée du matin ; Londres.

10 Hill Road, Abbey Road, London, G.B.

1909 – (SAF) 1648 - Australia Felix.

1909 – (SNBA) 1101 - Sydney Harbor Australia.

1911 – (SAF) 1753 - Ariane.
1754 - Château Corfe.

1912 – (SAF) 1738 - Malham Cove (Yorkshire).

1913 – (SAF) 1697 - La vallée de Sir Richard Arkwright.

STRUTT Alfred William

Born 1856 Taranaki, NZ ; died March 8 1924 Wadhurst, Sussex, G.B.

Elève de W. Strutt. 54 rue Notre-Dame-des-Champs, chez M. Paul Foinet, Paris (6th)

1897 – (SAF) 1594 - Savoir bon gré.
4414 - Si Taim – eau-forte.

Cher M. Graves et Cie, 18 rue de Caumartin, Paris (9th)

1908 – (SAF) 1719 - Dernière résistance.
1459 - Une gravure (burin) : Riche et pauvre.

Wadhurst, Sussex, G.B.

1909 – (SAF) 1649 – 'Chapeau dans l'air'.

1910 – (SAF)	4999 – 'C'est le premier pas qui coûte, d'après M. William Strutt', burin.
1912 – (SAF)	3112 – 'Mort aux machines', aquarelle.

SWAN Torfrida

Born Ballarat, Victoria ; (active : 1919-1938)

16 rue de la Grande-Chaumière, chez M. Castelucho, Paris (6th)

1923 – (TUILERIES)	969 - Paysage anglais.
1924 – (TUILERIES)	1451 - Fin de jour, aquarelle.
	1452 - La neige- entrée du village, aquarelle.
1928 – (TUILERIES)	2653 - Le lointain.
	2654 - Le Silence.
1929 – (TUILERIES)	1213 - Paysage.

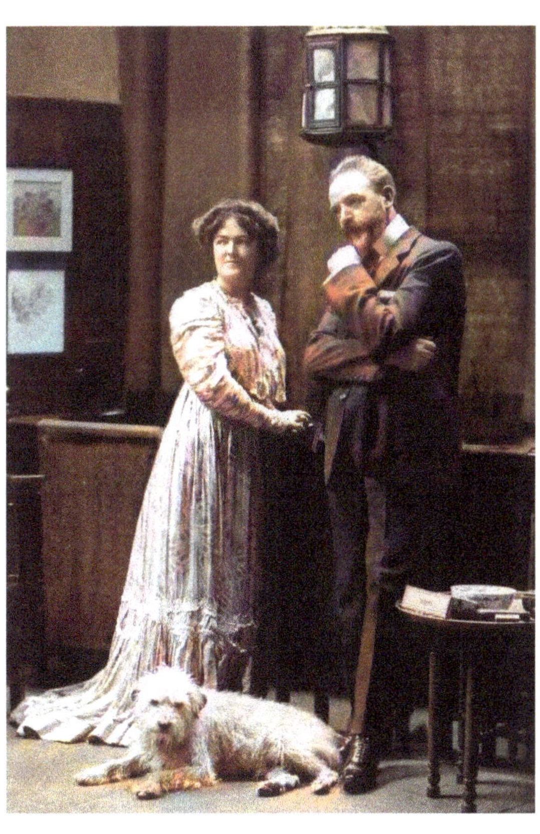

Nora and Arthur Streeton at their St Johns Wood home 1909.

T

TEAGUE Violet

Born 21 February 1872 Melbourne, Victoria, died 30 September 1951 Mount Eliza, Victoria.

1898 – (SAF)	1932 - Portrait de M. Robert Rede.

117 Finchley Road, chez C. H. West, London, G.B.

1923 – (SAF)	1624 - Jadis.
	1625 - La miniature de sa grand-mère.

THOMPSON J. L.

Born NZ.

Beuzer-Comq, Concarneau, Finistère, France.

1914 – (SNBA)	1141 - Marché (automne).
	1657 - Pêcheurs (design).

THOMPSON Nona Eugénie

Born Taihape, NZ .

Villa Riant-Séjour, Etaples, Pas-de-Calais, France.

1914 – (SNBA)	1142 - Nature morte.

THOMPSON Sydney Lough

Born 24 January 1877 Oxford, Canterbury, NZ, died 8 June 1973, Concarneau, France.

Elève de MM. Bouguereau et Gabriel Ferrier. Hôtel de Concarneau, Finistère, France.

1904 – (SAF)	1738 - Portrait.
	1739 - Au pardon.
	2567 - Pas assez, design.

23 quai Pénéroff, Concarneau, Finistère, France.

1922 – (SAF)	1755 - Au repos, Concarneau. (mention honorable)
	1756 - Arrivée des barques, Concarneau.
	1757 - Chargement des thons, Concarneau.

Saint-Jeannet, Alpes-Maritimes, France.

1923 – (SAF)	1648 - Sur la digue (Concarneau).

1649 - Arrivée des sardiniers.
1650 - Le matin.

18 rue Cadet, chez M. Reitz, Paris (9th)

1924 – (SAF) 1900 - Portrait.
1901 - Mon jardin.
1902 - Port de Concarneau.
1903 - Le cheval blanc.

23, quai Pénéroff, Concarneau, Finistère, France.

1926 – (SAF) 1902 - A l'ombre.

Campagne La Mitou, quartier Saint-Antoine, Grasse, Alpes-Maritimes, France.

1927 – (SAF) 1812 - Matin Concarneau.
1813 - Soir Concarneau.

1931 – (SAF) 2127 - Lavoir en Provence.

1933 – (SAF) 2437 - La vallée.
2438 - La chaise verte.

TRAILL Jessie C. A.

Born 29 July 1881 Brighton, Victoria, died 15 May 1967 Emerald , Victoria.

Elève de M. Frank Brangwyn. Chez Mme Bouval, 27 avenue du Maine, Paris (14th)

1909 – (SAF) 4839 - Echafaudage à Londres, etching.

TUCK Isabella Mary Stuart

Born Parramatta, NSW.

25 rue de Longchamp, Paris (16th)

1909 – (SAF) 2870 - Portrait de M. Greer, miniature.

Elève de Mme Laforge, de MM. Devina et Gervex. 5 rue Lord-Byron, Paris (8th)

1910 – (SAF) 3146 - Portrait de Mme Guterbock , miniature.
3147 - Vera P… , miniature.

Elève de Mme Laforge et de M. Delécluse. 5 rue Lord-Byron, Paris (8th).

1912 – (SAF) 3097 - Portrait de la comtesse X… ,miniature.

3098 - Portrait de M. Brton, fils du Rev. Anstruther-Cardaw , miniature.

1913 – (SAF) 3007 - Portrait d'Eric-W. Perrin, miniature.

TUCK Marie Anne

Born 5 September 1866 Mount Torrens, SA, died 3 September1947 Adelaide, SA.

Elève de M. Bunny. 55 rue du Montparnasse, Paris (6th)

1908 – (SAF) 1823 - Les commères.

1824 - La poissonnerie.

1909 – (SAF) 1741 - Jour de lessive.

Elève de M. Rupert Bunny. 55 rue du Montparnasse, Paris (6th)

1910 – (SAF) 1808 - Sortie des premières communiantes.

1910 – (AUTOMNE) 1155 - Les Couturières bretonnes.

1156 - Intérieur breton.

1911 – (SAF) 1841 - Gavotte d'honneur. (mention honorable)

1842 - Toilette de la mariée.

Elève de M. Rupert Bunny. 55 rue du Montparnasse, et chez M. Lucien Lefebvre-Foinet, 2 rue Bréa, Paris (6th)

1912 – (SAF) 1818 - La passante.

Amis des arts. 60e expo. Elève de M. Rupert Bunny. Ment. hon. A Paris, 55 rue du Montparnasse, Paris (6th)

1912 – (BORDEAUX) 616 - La repasseuse (400 fr)

617 - Les couturières (350 fr)

19 rue Vavin, chez M. L. Foinet, Paris (6th), et boulevard Billiet, Etaples-sur-Mer, Pas-de-Clais, France.

1913 – (SAF) 1776 - Un jour de fête à Etaples.

1914 – (SAF) 1958 - Halles aux poissons à Etaples.

TUCKER Tudor Saint George

Born 18 April 1862 Finchley, Middlesex G.B, died 21 December 1906 London, G.B.

Elève de M. J.-P. Laurens. Rue des Beaux-Arts, hôtel de Nice, Paris (6th)

1891 – (SAF) 1616 - Une pêcheuse de crevettes.

Elève de MM. Bouguereau, T. Robert-Fleury, Gérôme et Ferrier.
Etaples, Pas-de-Calais, France.

1892 – (SAF) 1624 - Un appel pressant.
15 Grove End Road, London, G.B.

1906 – (SAF) 1641 - Une première communiante.

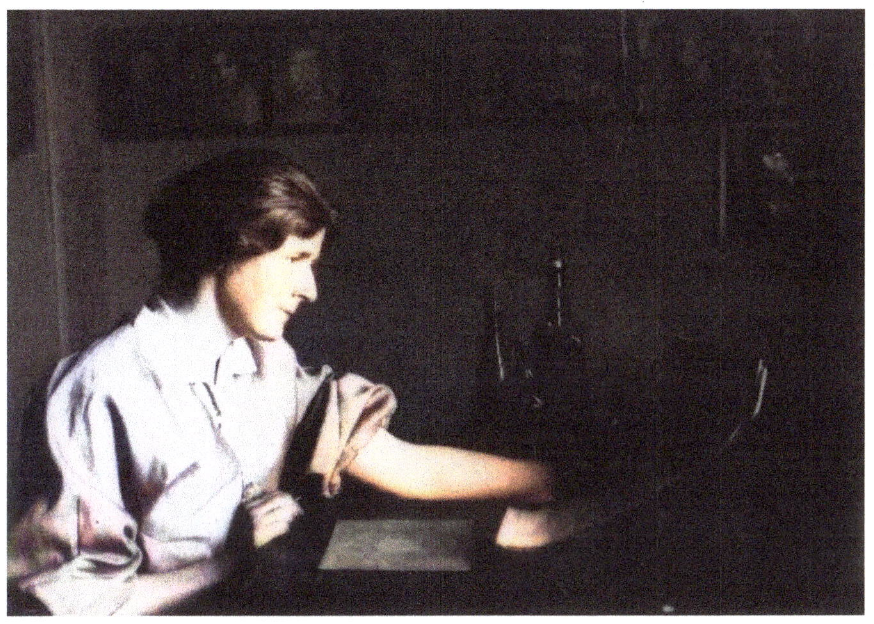

Jessie Traill, proofing an etching in subdued light, 1920.

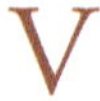

VYNER Madeleine
Born Dunedin, NZ, died Christchurch, NZ.
23 rue Serpente, Paris (6th)

1937 – (INDEPENDANTS)
3213 - Danse – Appartient à l'auteur.
3214 - La Terre Rouge renaît en dansant (1500 fr)

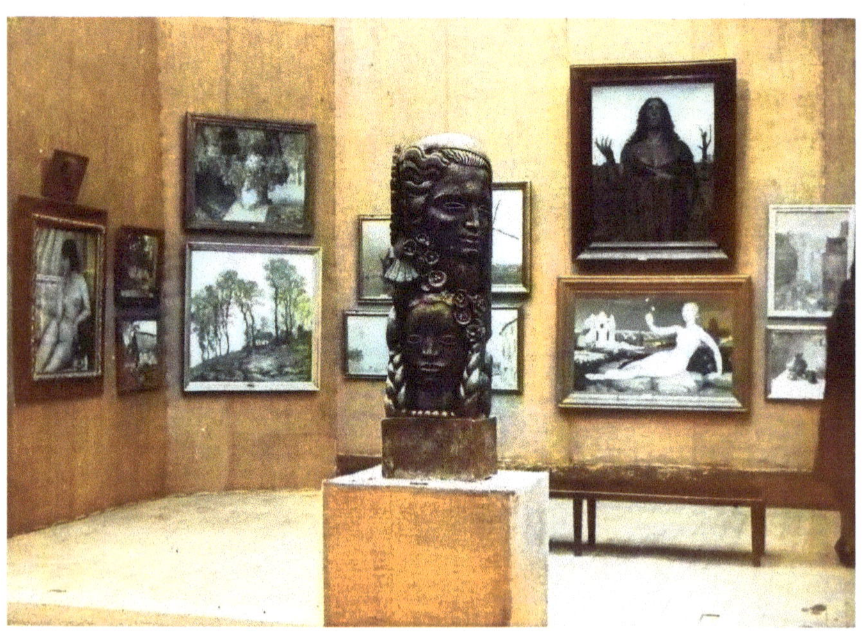

Part of the exhibition of the 1933 Salon des Independants.

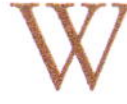

WATERLOW Hinemoa Pukoia
Born 1891 Auckland

22 Norfolk Road, London, G.B.

1923 – (SAF) 1722 - Portrait de M. V. Thomas.
1924 – (SDAI) 3105 - Mme Eva Jewell (portrait).
3106 - Le Tofane dans le Tyrol (Paysage), aquarelle (500 fr)
1926 – (SAF) 1993 - Portrait de M. Tack Kahane.
1994 - Marcelle.

36 Steele's Road, London, G.B.

1937 – (SAF) 1274 - Chanticleer.

WATSON Jeanie G.
Born in Australia.

Elève de MM. Ed. Krug et Feyen-Perrin. 29 boulevard des Batignolles, Paris (8th)

1887 – (SAF) Portrait de Mme Veuve Ange Tissier, design.

29 boulevard des Batignolles, Paris (8th).

1890 – (SAF) Portrait de Mme R, design.

WATSON Mabel
Born Sydney, NSW.

5 rue Léopold-Robert, Paris (14th)

1901 – (SAF) 2044 - La chaussure neuve.

WOOLRIYCH Francis Humphrey W.
Born 1868 in Sydney, NSW, died 1941 St. Louis, USA.

Elève de MM. R. Collin et Courtois. 26 Passage des Favorites, Paris. (15th)

1887 – (SAF) 2492 - Portrait.

Elève de MM. R. Collin, Courtois et Dagnan-Bouveret. 10 rue de la Grande-Chaumière, Paris (6th)

1888 – (SAF) 2553 - Portrait de Mlle C. H...

WILSON Nell
Born 1901 Melbourne, Victoria, died 1985
18 West Cromwell Road, London, G.B.
1935 – (SAF) 2308 - Fraga, Espagne.

WRIQUT Anna
Born in Australia.
17 rue Campagne-Première, Paris
1894 – (SAF) 1688 - Cinq miniatures.

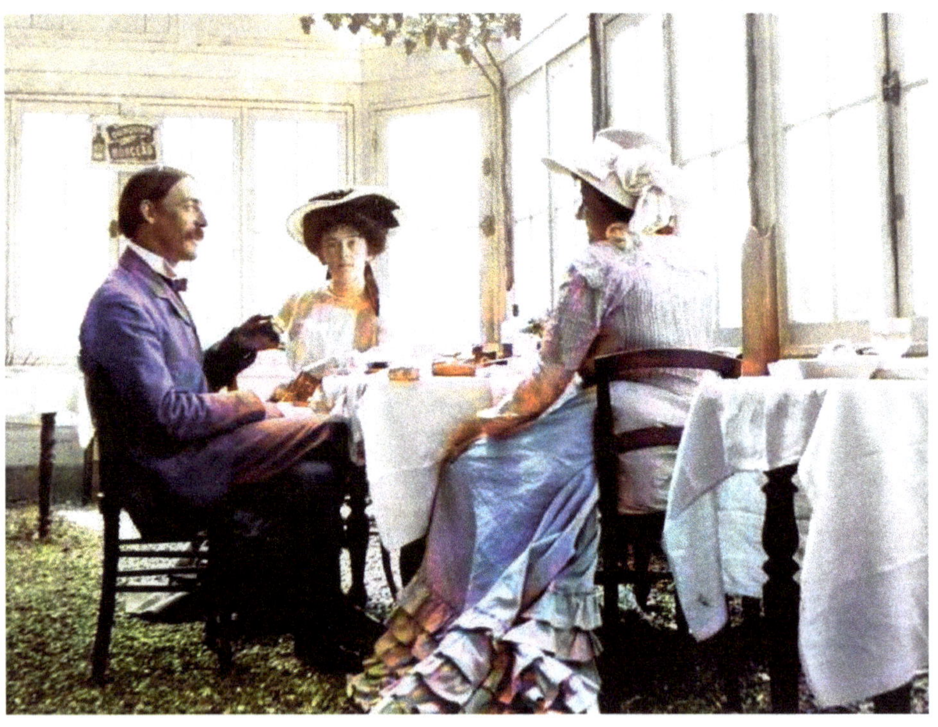

Charles Conder having tea with his wife Stella and Florence Humphrey at Les Petit Dalles, Normandy 1902.

TEA IN THE SALONS

More than two thousand British artists, nearly fourteen thousand works exhibited in the Salons, and all that in Paris alone, enough to change a few generally accepted ideas. While for nearly two and a half centuries the French were able to examine the art from the other side of the Channel, they continued to consider that it had never crossed this narrow strip of sea. It is surprising that British art should still remain today a rare field of interest for the French art historians. This repertory will avoid uncertain debates, and offers arguments, dry but irrefutable, on the subject of British artistic presence in France. One can measure almost mathematically the waves of influence, the literary echoes, the sources of inspiration. One can also measure the lessening role of the Salons as they multiply, not because the exhibited works are without merit but the Salons themselves no longer have the same impact.

To establish a list of British artists and their works exhibited in the Parisian salons is to show up the most publicly visible art of an epoch. Unlike the private collections, private exhibitions and the showrooms of art dealers, the Salons were frequented by an immense public which can be counted in tens of thousands. Even if every work of art was not looked at it was at least seen. The increasing number of works, the progressive disappearance of juries, the multiplication of Salons diminished their impact on the reputation of artists. Prints, photography, then the art dealers, the museums and exhibitions, did more for their glory than the Salons themselves. In spite of these reservations, the study of the *livrets* over such a long period allows us to define the main transformations.

This dictionary of British painters exhibiting in the main Parisian Salons from their beginnings up to 1940 is both an achievement and a start. An achievement certainly for its author and for the author of this essay, but it is also certainly the beginning of a reassessment of British art, in this case painting, in its relationship with France, and more widely with the rest of the world. English art has always been regarded as a somewhat strange artistic expression, not secondary but somewhat unusual, too unusual sometimes even to be taken into account. Its late genesis, its marked singularities, its strong literary aspects, have caused it to be viewed almost detached from the rest of European art. It has only been studied, as it were, by British art historians who have themselves harboured mixed feelings for it. These same British scholars have always admitted, with a wry smile expressing regret, contrition and a certain condescendence, the inferiority of their country's art, compared with that of Italy, France, Flanders, Holland, Spain. At the same time, they cultivated the idea that it could only be understood by the British themselves. Over the last few years this situation has changed rapidly. To the increasing number of British and American art historians can be added henceforth, in a homeopathic way certainly, a few non-Anglo-Saxon art historians. More material but determining aspects, when it is a question of research, must be mentioned : the support of the twin institutions of the Yale Center for British Art and the Paul Mellon Centre of London. One can never say enough to what an extent these wonderful institutions have counted in the elaboration of the history of British art and its high standard. No other school has benefited from a more efficient, regular and devoted support. The very nature of the research where perfect scholarship, the taste for attribution, the effects of the teachings of Francis Haskell, in the fields of painting, sculpture and decorative arts, of architecture and in the study of the great houses, and of the less-great ones, in their social, historical, literary and political aspects have lead scholars to a level rarely achieved for other schools of painting. Whilst British art was, and still is, considered as the poor relation of European art, its study has excelled, and not only in its discretion. There nevertheless remains a domain were the studies are in their infancy, that of the links with the continent, not the continental influences on the insular art but, on the contrary, the influence of the latter on the arts of the continent. From the middle of the 18th century onwards, England was the most innovatory country, as far as artistic trends were concerned Neoclassicism, the Gothic Revival, landscape painting, Romanticism, Symbolism owe so much to its inventiveness. Few continental art historians say it yet[1] and one should anticipate, one day, that what Louis Dussieux and Louis Réau did for French art should be done for British art. The only period really studied in this field remains that of the years 1820-1840 with the influence of Bonington and of Constable on French painting. From time to time there were studies of the influence of English painters on Goya, and research, still too fragmentary, on the English influence on 18th century Italy, on the Anglo-German relationships during these same years, but in fact it constitutes little compared with the breadth of the subject. There remain fields to be opened up as vast as they are fascinating as, for example, the influence of Hogarth on European art, Gavin Hamilton and the French, Reynolds in Europe, the relationships between the French and English artists in Italy during the second half of the 18th century, the influence of English Palladianism on Neoclassical European architecture, the diffusion of the English Neo-Gothic style, English literature and European art, Wedgwood and France, the anglophilia of the Orléans family, etc. . . It is evident that subjects of research abound from the general to the particular, from the essential to the accessory. This dictionary will at least allow the Franco-British relationships to be studied more easily.

THE GENESIS OF A DICTIONARY

This work is the fruit of a considerable amount of work which its readers will be able to measure at each page. It is also the result of a long evolution. Started in 1996, at the beginning it was only a review of the Parisian Salons of the year 1910! I had asked Béatrice Crespon to complete it. She was then on an assignment in the *Département des peintures* of the Louvre Museum, in order to prepare an exhibition of English painting of the period 1910-1940 which was to take place in the *Musée des Années 30*, at Boulogne-Billancourt and at the *Musée de Roubaix*. A long chapter of the exhibition catalogue was to be devoted to the rich Franco-British relations of the period. The exhibition was cancelled a few months before its

1 Jean Locquin in *La peinture d'histoire en France de 1747 à 1785*, Paris, 1912.

with the evident interest of this review, I convinced the author to continue her work until 1940, still hoping that an exhibition would allow the publication of the main part. At that time, Brian Allen, Director of the Mellon Centre for Studies in British Art in London, suggested, very logically, that the dictionary should be one where all the British painters having exhibited in the Parisian Salons from the beginnings of the Salon until 1940, be listed. Moreover, the intellectual and financial aid of the Paul Mellon Centre was determining as was the Documentation Centre of the Musée d'Orsay, which welcomed Béatrice Crespon during several months, as did the *Service de Documentation* and the Library of the *Département des Peintures* of the Louvre Museum.

Today the dictionary is complete, or almost. Certainly there are omissions, mistakes, artists wrongly included or excluded by inadvertence. Anyone who has worked on the *livrets* of the 19th and 20th century salons knows their complexity and their wealth, making such a task even more commendable. It represents the very type of project that we know is necessary without ever having the courage to undertake it. One needs both rigour and self-sacrifice, modesty and clear-sightedness and, above all, formidable perseverance. Its author had all that at only 222 years of age, her age in 1996. This realization also shows that the age of compilation is not past. The digitisation of the documents, even though it is undoubtedly useful and admirable, will not replace, before many years, this type of work. To extract from fastidious lists the artists of this or that nationality remains a task of discernment, precision, that of a historian. The analyses that one can draw are certainly numerous, but one in particular imposes itself. The number of British artists having exhibited in Paris during this century and a half is impressive, it is itself an indication of the vitality of these strange relationships maintained between our two countries. The number of works exhibited forbids us to ignore the place of British art in our visual culture.

I am sure that one will quote this dictionary in numerous articles and the name of its author will become, I hope, a household word for the small circle of art historians of British art. This dictionary will be used as a basis for the study of the Anglo-French relationships, but also for every study of the painting of Australia, South-Africa, India . . . The list is as long as that of the members of the Commonwealth. Some will be surprised to note the absence of American artists, a logical part of a dictionary of Anglo-Saxon painters. This choice is deliberate and has several reasons. The first, political or aesthetic, stems from the early independence of the United States and the establishment of a different national tradition. The most determining is the existence of a dictionary of American artists who exhibited in the French salons for the years 1800-1899[2]. It seemed to us unnecessary to double an already remarkable piece of work. The dictionary of Lois Marie Fink, which figures as an annexe to a long and remarkable reflection on the subject, demonstrates that the American participation was also considerable. During a century, nearly a thousand American artists, painters, draughtsmen, or sculptors exhibited nearly five thousand works. For these reasons, Béatrice Crespon has compiled a repertory of the artists of the British Empire.

The repertory is arranged alphabetically by artist and not chronologically by date of Salon. The chronological evolution would show more and more numerous artists and an increasing proportion of women, an aspect that has no equivalent in other national participations[3]. From a purely artistic point of view, it should also be noted that, apart from a few famous exceptions (John Martin) and national selections for *Expositions Universelles*, the British artists of high reputation were loath to send their works to the Paris salons. Thus Constable was not yet established when he yielded to the offers of Arrowsmith, Lawrence was almost on an official mission, and if a little later Ford Madox Brown submitted a work in 1842, it was before being famous. This state of affairs was only to be confirmed in the following decades. The British artists who show in Paris when they are well established are often fashionable in worldly circles. It is nonetheless true that two thousand artists came across the Channel and from overseas to show thousands of works in Paris, and apart from a few precise episodes, this presence has been little studied. It is therefore necessary to benefit from this essay to try and paint a panorama of this British presence and its evolution.

2 Lois Marie Fink, *American art at the Nineteenth-Century Paris Salons,* Washington, Cambridge University Press, 1990.

3 Béatrice Crespon, 'British Painters in the Paris Salons, 1881-1939, A real presence', *The British Art Journal,* 2000, Spring, Vol. 1, n°2, p. 59-61.

THE SALONS DURING THE ANCIEN RÉGIME, THE REVOLUTION AND THE EMPIRE : REFUSAL OF FOREIGNERS

Unlike the *Accademia di San Luca in Rome*, and the *Royal Academy* in London, the *Académie Royale de Peinture et de Sculpture* of Paris did not tolerate the presence of foreigners at the Salons. This situation continued during the Revolution and the Empire. The foreign artists present during this period were generally from conquered countries which only gives a limited idea of opening to the rest of the world. The only Salon that foresaw the presence of foreigners was that of 1791. Unfortunately no foreign artist seems to have expressed the desire to take part. One should however note the presence during the Salons of the Revolution of several foreign artists such as the Dane Jean-Pierre Pfab in the 1798 and 1799 salons, of Henriette Rab and Töpfer from Switzerland and of Serangeli, the Roman. No English artists can be found in the Salon before 1815 with the exception of Benjamin West in 1802, a presence decided for purely diplomatic reasons and the wishes of Bonaparte without whom nothing was decided. The painting that West chose to exhibit came as a surprise for the French. The artist had been celebrated in France for over forty years for his Neo-classical compositions inspired by Roman history and sculpture in friezes. The French, then under the artistic domination of David, expected that he would send some great heroic composition aesthetically inherited from Winckelmann and Gavin Hamilton. They were disappointed, surprised by a biblical subject, taken moreover from the Apocalypse and above all treated in a manner nearer to Rubens than to Poussin. One can assume that Benjamin West's choice was not innocent, placing in front of the eyes of the French, then under a regicidal and atheistic regime, a royal command from King George III, a religious composition intended for the private chapel of the sovereign. After the Peace of Amiens, the war started again and the experience was not repeated.

Before approaching one of the richest periods of exchange in the history of the French Salons we must look back at the presence of British painting in France before the Revolution[4]. This absence from the annual Parisian Salons should not lead us into thinking that no English artist showed his work in France before this date. First of all in Paris, thanks to

[4] An article on this subject should appear in 2003 in a supplement of the *British Art Journal*, its follows two lectures given by the author on this subject the 17 May 2001 at the Yale Center for British Art, Newhaven CT, and on January 9, 2002, at the Sorbonne University, Paris.

Pahin de la Blancherie and his *Salon de la Correspondance* where several English artists exhibited. In addition he wrote regular accounts of the Annual Exhibitions of the Royal Academy in London in his *Journal.* But it was also in the French provinces that one could find several English artists. These provincial salons were often exhibitions where works of old masters were mixed with those of contemporary artists, showing works from private collections and the works of local artists both modest and famous. These exhibitions also illustrate the noteworthy openness of the French provinces in the second half of the 18th century. When one examines the *livrets* of the Salons of Montpellier, of Toulouse or of Lille, one is agreeably surprised to find artists from across the Channel and not the least, Reynolds for example, was represented by two works in the Salon of Montpellier in 1779[5].

In the Salons of Lille names such as Luckock, Beagle or Charles Woodington appear, but they are above all pupils showing copies after the masters[6].

The most perfect example is that of Toulouse. Thanks to the publication of the 18th century Salons of Toulouse by Robert Mesuret in 1972[7], it is possible to measure the presence of British artists in a French region which could only claim to have very ancient links, broken in the distant past, with Great Britain. No famous artists as was the case in Montpellier, but artists passing through or works belonging to collectors from Toulouse. In 1768, James Alvès (1738-1808), a Scottish painter who had been converted to Roman Catholicism during his stay in Rome, miniaturist, who was staying at that time in Toulouse, presented a portrait[8]. In 1772, several portraits by Lewis[9], and another miniaturist "recently arrived in this town", showed their works. These works were then the property of the comte de Bournazel. In 1776, Cammas showed three works by William Taverner (1703-1772), an important English landscape painter,

5 Henri Stein, op. cit., p. 365-402.

6 *Les Salons de Lille* : Mr Luckock, Anglois, élève de l'Ecole de dessin, p. 67 ; Mr Beagle le cadet, élève de l'Ecole de dessin, p. 163 ; Charles Woodington, élève de l'Ecole de dessin, p. 261, 281, 305, 326. Cf. J. Lefèbvre, *Livrets des Salons de Lille (1773-1788),* Paris-Lille, 1882. Réédition à Nogent-le-Roi, J. Laget, 1995.

7 Robert Mesuret, *Les expositions de l'Académie Royale de Toulouse de 1751 à 1791*, Toulouse, 1972.

8 Robert Mesuret, op. cit., p. 189.

9 Perhaps J.Lewis (active in England in 1744), one of the rare known miniatures by this artist is moreover in the *Département des Arts Graphiques* of the Louvre Museum.

coming from his private collection[10]. In 1783 it was a painting by Joshua Boydell (1752-1817)[11] "Des voyageurs se rafraîchissant" from the cabinet of the Marquis de Fourquevaux which was exhibited[12].

RULE BRITANNIA, 1815-1855

The most favourable period for artistic exchanges between the two countries was, without doubt, that of the Restoration and of the July Monarchy. Numerous factors facilitated this situation. The first was probably the English victory over France. Our country, after defeats, often tried to understand the reasons for the superiority of the conqueror and this in all domains. We saw this same tragic curiosity after the 1870 Franco-Prussian war, when we tried to revivify our country, not only in the fields of education, the army, and social relationships but also in the arts and music, inspired by the German successes. Even though this Franco-German episode has been studied, that of England remains to be explored, going beyond simple notions of anglophilia. Another reason for the interest shown in England was certainly the stays, more or less prolonged, of the French *émigrés* in England during the Revolution. Emigration is a phenomenon little studied in France and often considered only from a political point of view, often reducing and negative. The most recent studies often carried out by Anglo-Saxons show that emigration can often play a very positive role in the relationships between two countries[13]. The return to a country of a population that had been in contact with a more democratic political system, a different religion, other literary ideas and artistic trends, was particularly beneficial and should not be reduced to the famous formula "nothing forgotten and nothing learnt". The success of British literature during this first part of the century is a sign of French receptiveness to the literary and artistic manifestations coming from the other side of the Channel[14].

---

10 Robert Mesuret, op. cit., p. 299.

11 Nephew of John, the famous commissioner of the *Shakespeare Gallery*, Joshua Boydell showed paintings at the Royal Academy and at the Society of Artists.

12 Robert Mesuret, op. cit., p. 414.

13 Kirsty Carpenter, *Refugees of the French Revolution, émigrés in London, 1789-1802*, New York, 1999.

14 In particular for Walter Scott and Byron but also for an artist such as John Martin (Jean Seznec, *John Martin en France*, London, Faber and Faber, 1964).

From the strict point of view of painting, the most famous episode remains that of the 1824 Salon. It has incited an abundant literature which has highlighted the contribution of Constable to French landscape painting and, more broadly, the contribution of English painters to the renewal of French aesthetics[15].

This period is, however, the best studied. The studies on Bonington, Constable, Turner, John Martin and more generally on the artistic Anglo-French links have largely cleared the ground[16]. One should, however, emphasize the English presence before the 1824 Salon. The first noteworthy artist who exhibited was John Crome whose work and influence have always been underestimated in France. He exhibited in 1815, he worked in France and his work was well known. In French collections many paintings proudly bear the name of this Norwich painter, but rarely rightly. These paintings are a proof of his fame during the whole of the 19th century.

In the same way, Thomas Lawrence, enjoyed a real glory and painted several portraits at the court and in the town. Certain paintings by Lawrence were famous all over France, even in modest dwellings. They were portraits of children whose main attraction was their gentleness. Their identities were secondary. The official portraits that he painted of King Charles X, of the duc d'Angoulême, the latter superb, and of the duchesse de Berry were successful as were their models. His portrait of the duc de Richelieu, shown in the Salon of 1824, commissioned by the sister of the model, after the painting of the Congress of Vienna, occupies a special place[17]. To the Parisian exhibitions should be added, one must mention once more, the exhibitions in the provinces, especially in the North of

---

15 Basil Long, 'The Salon of 1824', *Connoisseur*, February 1924, p. 66-76 ; Michel Floorisone, 'Constable and the Massacre of Scio by Delacroix', in the *Journal of the Warburg and Courtauld Institutes*, vol. XX, n°1-2, 1957.

16 Prosper Dorbec, 'Les paysagistes anglais en France', *Gazette des Beaux Arts*, 1912, II, p. 257-281 ; Jean Adhémar, *Les lithographies de paysage en France à l'époque romantique*, Paris, Armand Colin, 1937 ; Marcia Pointon, *Bonington, Francia & Wyld*, London, Victoria and Albert Museum, 1985 ; Patrick Le Nouëne et al., *Louis Francia 1772-1839*, Calais, 1988 ; Patrick Noon, *Richard Parkes Bonington 'Du plaisir de peindre'*, Paris, Petit Palais, 1992 ; The thesis unfortunately as yet unpublished of Barthélemy Jobert on '*La réception de l'école anglaise en France, 1802-1878*', Paris, Sorbonne Paris IV, 1995 ; Olivier Meslay, 'Les peintres de Barbizon et l'Angleterre', in *L'Ecole de Barbizon, peindre en plein-air avant l'impressionnisme*, catalogue of the exhibition at Lyon, June 22 – September 9, 2002, p. 54 to 65.

17 Olivier Meslay, 'Sir Thomas Lawrence and France, the portrait of the duc de Richelieu', The British Art Journal, Spring, 2002, vol.III, n°2, p. 44-49.

France[18], thus relaying outside the capital the successes obtained in the *Salon Carré* on the Louvre Museum. The last artist to experience renown from the Salon, John Martin, was appreciated in particular by writers even more than by artists. The cabinet of John Martin, which is kept in the Museum of Newcastle, bears on one of its drawers the name of Charles X associated with the Paris Salons. This moving relic brings a new proof of the importance of the Salon for the diffusion of English art in France.

After the years 1820-1830, English painting, which had become customary, took its place in French culture. Whilst the critics and the artists seemed to have assimilated the novelties of British art, a new shock, quite different, took place during the Exposition of 1855[19]. The Pre-Raphaelites appeared. Only Ford Madox Brown had shown his works in Paris previously - in 1842, some six years before the foundation of the Brotherhood. This new movement was to incite deep perplexity. Neither the manner, nor the theories which were at the basis of this painting, was really understood. Edmond About, otherwise a well-informed critic of the *Exposition des Beaux-Arts* of the *Exposition Universelle* of 1855, does not perceive the importance of the movement. He comments profusely the ensemble of the British productions, and writes at length on Sir George Hayter, William Mulready, William Powell Frith, Sir Edwin Landseer, giving the same attention, but no more, to the works of John Everett Millais, William Dyce and Holman Hunt. For the last-named his commentary is as follows : *The* Light of the World, *and* Strayed Sheep (Our English Coasts), *by the same artist, are two precious paintings, precious in the meaning that they show to what an extent the taste of the painter can lead to aberrations. This painting, learnedly hideous, should have a place of its own. One should have created for it a Chamber of Horrors, as one has done in the wax-work gallery of Madame Tussaud - this object of eternal admiration of the idlers of London*[20].

---

18 Annette Haudiquet, *Les salons retrouvés : éclat de la vie artistique dans la France du nord 1815-1848*, Association des Conservateurs des Musées du Nord-Pas-de-Calais, 1993.

19 Cf. Dominique Lobstein, 'L'Exposition universelle des Beaux-Arts de 1855', dans P. Sanchez et X. Seydoux, *Les Catalogues des Salons (1852-1857)*, Dijon, 2002, p.9-25.

20 Edmond About, *Voyage à travers l'exposition des Beaux-Arts*, Paris, 1855, p.26-27. See also, for example, Maxime du Camp, *L'Exposition universelle de 1855*, Paris, p. 15-16 ; Théophile Gautier, *Les Beaux-Arts en Europe*, Paris, 1855.

Edmond About concludes his chapter on the English section by a passage in which he notes : *To sum up, the English school is the only one in the world that does not stem from ours and that has kept a strong originality. It shows more spirit than imagination, more science than talent, more meticulousness than vigour, more draughtsmanship than colour.* He continues by taking up the usual accusation of mercantilism so often associated with the English in French spirit of the 19th century : *Such as it is, the English school obtains an enormous financial success throughout the United Kingdom. Its products are much sought-after, it augments its prices, demand cannot be satisfied. The nation is insatiable; in order to pay for these paintings it uses up all its economies. In England painting is, for those who buy it, the highest degree of luxury, and for those who make it, the highest degree of industry.*

In fact, one has to wait until the end of the century and the noteworthy Robert de La Sizeranne[21] in order to read a really pertinent analysis of Pre-Raphaelite painting of the first and second generation. First of all, Sizeranne makes the same analysis as About by underlining the English distinctive characteristics, but he comes to quite different conclusions. He writes, concerning the innumerable international exhibitions : *As long as one walks through the rooms devoted to Germany, Austria, Italy, Spain, Belgium, Holland, even the United States, one feels still in France . . . One needs a number of written explanations to be persuaded that the Atlantic Ocean exists between M. Sargent and the studio of M. Carolus Duran.* Concerning the English, he writes : *The British Isles, on the contrary, contrast violently with the rest of the world. Their painters seem to ignore that there is a continent . . . the waves of realism, of impressionism, break on the walls of their aesthetics like the squadrons of Ney on the massed troops of Wellington. There are German, Hungarian, Belgian, Spanish, Scandinavian painters, but there is an English school of painting.* Unlike About, he admires the English profoundly and the art that they had created outside the continental norms. Sizeranne had read Ruskin and he quotes in his book extracts from *Modern Painters.* He could also explain better the prejudices of the Pre-Raphaelite painters. That of their meticulousness which found, for example, a motto in the phrase of Ruskin : *If Nature realises minutiae over*

21 Robert de La Sizeranne, *La peinture anglaise contemporaine*, Paris, 1895.

several miles, (the painter) has no excuse for making generalisations over a few square inches.

The 1855 Exhibition marked in a certain way the end of a period in Franco-British relations. After the enthusiasm of the 1824 Salon a period of relative interest followed only broken by some passions kept alive in restricted circles by a few refined amateurs.

A PERMANENT PRESENCE AND A CERTAIN INDIFFERENCE, 1855-1910

The second half of the 19th century and the first years of the 20th show, in a certain way, a pause in the Franco-British relations. The links are henceforth established politically, economically and in literature. Universal exhibitions regularly recall the weight of England in all fields. Colonial competition did not really harm the good relationships of a cool *entente cordiale*. Napoléon III knew London and England well, he hadn't discovered them, he had been brought up there. His son was to die wearing a British uniform without feeling betrayal.

Whilst the Parisian urbanism of the Second Empire and the Third Republic was to be changed completely by an English vision imposed by Napoléon III, and later by the Parisian and provincial councillors, painting was not to undergo the same influence. French symbolists were sometimes to look across the Channel, a few amateurs were to be enthusiastic about the Pre-Raphaelites of the second generation, but they were not very numerous[22]. What is more striking is the taste shown by the French *élite* for the 18th century English painting. This passion followed its discovery after the exhibition *Art Treasures* in Manchester in 1857. From then on it was the done thing to have a Reynolds, a Gainsborough, a Romney. A few daring amateurs like Cheramy and Groult, who could even be considered as eccentric, were enthusiastic about Constable. Camille Groult, whose taste for English art became a passion, even created, for a certain time, a museum of English art at Bagatelle[23] to compensate the departure of the French

22 Philippe Saunier, 'Edward Burne-Jones et la France : Madeleine Deslands, une préraphaélite oubliée', *Revue de l'Art*, n°123, 1999-1, p. 57-70. Laurence des Cars, *Les Préraphaélites, un modernisme à l'anglaise*, Paris, 1999. Philippe Saunier, 'Les préraphaélites anglais. Les reproductions de leurs œuvres et leur réception au XIXe siècle en France', *Revue de l'Art*, n°137, 2002-3, p. 73-86.

23 Arsène Alexandre, 'Un musée à Bagatelle', in *Les Arts*, June 1905, n°42.

treasures of the Wallace Collection. This competition was to end with the closing of the museum, but English art was considered worthy of being shown. This was also the time of the first enrichments of the French public collections as it is of the first French publications on English art. Once more it is the art of the past that is privileged by the authors whilst modern and contemporary art are neglected. Alone, the work of Robert de La Sizeranne on contemporary English painting stands out. For the first time a Frenchman develops an original theory on British art, both carefully worked out and pertinent. It is not an arranged version of thoughts conceived elsewhere but a French analysis of English art. It was probably the first time that this had happened on such a scale and with such a knowledge and such a depth of view. What is striking in this work in that the understanding rests neither on complacent admiration nor on renouncement of criticism.

Apart from this exception, English art at this time incites but little interest. The prodigious years of French art, the first Impressionist exhibitions and the *Salons Fauves*, occupy French minds enough for the need to go elsewhere to find novelty not to be felt. When the French looked outside their frontiers it was generally to look for and find confirmation of the excellence and radiant influence of French art, rarely to find exceptions to their leadership.

Paradoxically, this period finds its epilogue with two exhibitions organised by Roger Fry in London in 1910 and 1912. These exhibitions on Post-Impressionism in France had a considerable repercussion in Great Britain and partly broke the introspection of the British artists. It might appear surprising to end the study of a particular period of British presence in the Paris Salons with these London manifestations. but the event undeniably marks a change in the Franco-British relations and, in particular, the international artistic relationships.

1911-1939, THE DISTANCE BETWEEN BROTHERS IN ARMS

Roger Fry and his friends thought that they had succeeded but one has to admit today that British art remained impermeable to influence from the continent, and in particular during the first half of the 20th century.

How bizarre the 1938 exhibition in the *Salon des Indépendants* must have appeared to all. What strange art, figurative, without being traditional, not really influenced by international trends, but fully aware of worldwide currents through personalities such as Roland Penrose and Herbert Read and many other first rank figures. It is probable that one will not really understand the nature of 20th century art until English art from 1910 to 1940 is integrated into it. Still today, only Henry Moore, Barbara Hepworth and Ben Nicholson are quoted in the histories of world art. Stanley Spencer is almost never considered and all the others are unknown. It is perhaps however in Great Britain that one can find the last national school, not as a survival of the past but as a true motor of invention. For the moment, its insularity has left it outside the field of studies, but when it has found its place it will shed light in a singular way on the whole of modern art analyses.

As far as Franco-British relations are concerned, there has probably been no period in the history of the two nations that has brought them so closely together, firstly by the blood shed in the trenches of the First World War and then on the beaches of Dunkirk and Normandy, in the proximity of the literary élites as one can read in the writings of André Maurois and André Gide. In artistic matters this proximity is not translated into facts. Apart from several individual relationships, in particular within the Surrealist Movement, the links in the field of painting are distended. Nonetheless, all should have contributed to their coming together. British painters exhibiting in the Parisian Salons were never so numerous as at that time. Exhibitions organised by art dealers include works by English artists, and the finest foreign section of the Luxembourg Museum is that of England, in particular thanks to the very generous donation of Sir Edmund Davis.

This donation to the Luxembourg Museum, with the full agreement of its curator, Léonce Bénédite, allowed the French public to get to know British painting better and thus to complete what they could see in the Salons. The collection, donated in 1915, included several works by the Pre-Raphaelites such as Sir Edward Burne-Jones, William Holman Hunt, Sir John Everett Millais, but above all those of contemporaries[24]. Among the

---

24 Olivier Meslay, 'La collection de Sir Edmund Davis', *48/14, La Revue du Musée d'Orsay*, n°8, printemps 1999, p. 40-49.

latter one should quote numerous painters who had never exhibited in the French Salons, such as Aubrey Beardsley, Robert Anning Bell, Eric H. Kennington, Ambrose Mac Evoy, Sir William Orpen, Glyn Philpot, James Ferrier Pryde, Arthur and Edith Rackham, Ferderick Cayley Robinson, William Strang and Henry Tonks. This list is interesting because it shows that the numerous works sent to the Salon are far from representative of all the artistic currents.

The two wars, and in particular the years that lead up to them, were particularly rich in English exhibitions in France. Each time that the conflicts with Germany approached, the two governments as well as the independent artistic organisations organised manifestations specially devoted to British art. During the First World War, there were many small exhibitions; during the years 1938-1939 there were other manifestations of a quite different scope. First of all there was the exhibition of *La Peinture Anglaise* which was held at the Louvre Museum in 1938 and which, in spite of its sub-title *XVIIIe et XIXe siècles*, showed certain almost contemporary works. The exhibition, which included no less than 330 works was colossal. To this important official retrospective exhibition another show was devoted to contemporary English painting, that of the private *L'Art anglais indépendant contemporain* which was held at the *Salon d'Automne* in 1938. It brought together the *fine fleur* of the British artistic scene. More than fifty artists were gathered together including : Richard Eurich, Mark Gertler, Eric Gill, Duncan Grant, Barbara Hepworth, Augustus John, Bernard Meninsky, Henry Moore, John Nash, Paul Nash, Ben Nicholson, Victor Pasmore, John Piper, Stanley Spencer, Graham Sutherland, Edward Wadsworth, to quote only a few of them[25]. Even though the selection was judicious, it showed the widening gap that had grown between the most innovative art of the United Kingdom and what was shown in the French Salons. Among all the artists who had been invited to take part in this manifestation, which owed much to the gathering storm of the war and to the political Franco-British alliance, only seven had previously shown works in Parisian salons. Vanessa Bell exhibited in 1921, Charles Ginner in 1912

---

[25] Olivier Meslay, « Exported art from Lowry to Spencer, British artists exhibiting in Paris 1900-1940 », *The British Art Journal*, 2000, Spring, vol. 1, n° 2, p. 55-58.

and 1913, Hodgkins in 1924, Cedric Morris in 1921, Ethel Walker in 1922 and 1923. The only artists who had sent works regularly to the Parisian salons were, without much surprise, given their close links with out country, Walter Sickert and Matthew Smith. This absence of important British artists in the Salons first of all indicates a certain disinterest of artists towards Salons. It can also be explained by the increasing divorce between a large part of British and International art. Even though Henry Moore had been annexed by the great abstract movements, this often took place thanks to a profound incomprehension of the roots of the art of the sculptor. In spite of all this important British figures exhibited in the French capital.

Important artists were to be found in private exhibitions in Paris devoted to them, like Edward Wadsworth, Christopher Wood or Ben Nicholson, who showed their works at the Bernheim Jeune Gallery. Group shows took place chez Barbazanges in 1912, under the title of *Les Indépendants anglais* and at the Durand Ruel Gallery in 1911 and 1927 already bringing together numerous artists who were to be shown at the *Salon d'Automne* in 1938.

We must not diminish, for all that, the interest of the Salons, as one can find some surprising exhibitors such as the Manchester painter L.S.Lowry, and the increasing presence of women painters can be measured[26]. Of course, artists such as Gwen John attracted admirers, and artists such as Laura Knight, who was well known in England, did not hesitate to show their works in Paris. This Anglo-Saxon attitude must have surprised French society which was still very conservative as to the place of women.

FRENCH PURCHASES OF BRITISH PAINTING IN THE PARIS SALONS

In order to conclude this survey of the British presence in the Paris Salons, it is perhaps not without interest to evoke the policy of acquisitions of the French state in these manifestations. A deeper study should soon be carried out, not only on the purchases by the state but also by private persons. It is, of course, difficult to carry out the latter.

---

26 Béatrice Crespon, British Painters in the Paris Salons 1881-1939, a real presence, *The British Art Journal*, printemps 2002, vol. 1, n°2, p. 55-58.

The most famous example of a purchase by private persons goes back to the 1824 Salon when two large paintings by Constable, *The Hay Wain* and *View on the Stour* were acquired. These purchases were made by private buyers even though the government had tried to buy one of them. The present state of research does not allow us to add any names to those of Coutan and of Boursault, the buyers of the masterpieces by Constable, and thus to shed light on the purchases by private collectors.

On the contrary, purchases by the State are easier to identify, even though a precise review has not yet been made, as it has for American painting[27]. The comparison that one can make between purchases of American painting and that of other western countries, including the United Kingdom, is moreover most interesting. It would appear that the Anglo-Saxon world had been favoured. For British painting, including that of Australia and Canada, nearly forty works were acquired in the different Salons. Moreover, it should be pointed out that purchases in private galleries or during exceptional manifestations have not been taken into account here. During the same period, the German and Spanish paintings counted together, acquired by the state, are less than ten, according to the first researches. studies.

As this is not the place to make a precise list of the works acquired by the State, I think that it is useful to show a summary list given chronologically[28] :

SAF	1894, John Henry Lorimer, *Bénédicité, fête de grand'mère.*
SAF	1895, Frank Brangwyn, *Marché sur la plage, Maroc.*
SAF	1896, John Henry Lorimer, *Le colonel Anstruther Thomson.*
SAF	1900, Sir John Lavery, *Père et fille.*
SAF	1900, Robert Sims, *L'enfance.*

[27] Véronique Wiesinger, La politique d'acquisition sous la troisième république en matière d'art étranger contemporain : l'exemple américain (1870-1940), *Bulletin de la Société de l'Art Français*, 1993, p. 263-299.

[28] This list owes much to the study of Caroline Ferreira which has unfortunately not been completed.

SAF	1901, Frank Spenlove-Spenlove, *Funérailles dans le Low Country, un jour d'hiver.*
SNBA	1902, Henry H. Brown, *Madame Boyd.*
SAF	1903, James Kay, *Une rivière du Nord.*
AUTOMNE	1904, Maxwell Armfield, *Faustine.*
SNBA	1904, Rupert C.W.Bunny, *Après le bain.*
SAF	1904, William Lee Hankey, *Toilette rustique.*
SAF	1904, Sir Herbert Hughes Stanton, *Port du Dorset.*
SNBA	1904, Sir John Lavery, *Printemps.*
SNBA	1904, James W.Morrice, *Quai des Grands Augustins.*
SAF	1904, Tom Robertson, *En Ecosse.*
SAF	1905, Frank Spenlove-Spenlove, *Le retour, trop tard.*
SAF	1906, Emmanuel P.Fox, *Rêverie.*
SAF	1908, Frank Craig, *La Pucelle, Jeanne d'Arc à la tête de son armée.*
SDAI	1911, Elizabeth F. Boyd, *Le Zitelle.*
SNBA	1912, Douglas F.Robinson, *Femme assise.*
SNBA	1913, Beatrice How, *Jean et l'orange.*
AUTOMNE	1913, Jeka Kemp, *La femme aux tulipes.*
SNBA	1914, Elizabeth F.Boyd, *Le salon à fresques.*
SAF	1914, Amy Katherine Browning, *le Châle rouge.*
SAF	1914, Cecil C.P.Lawson, *La sortie de Moscou, 1812.*
SAF	1914, William Lee Hankey, *La leçon de tricot.*
SAF	1914 John Young Hunter, *Le Rêve.*
SNBA	1914, Bertha Shore, *Le lit aux colonnes.*
SNBA	1915, Beatrice How, *Petites bretonnes.*
SAF	1918, Edward Chappel, *Effet nocturne.*
AUTOMNE	1920, Elizabeth Boyd, *Au bord de la mer, la fenêtre.*
SDAI	1920, Mabel Harrison, *La toilette.*
TUILERIES	1924, Bernard Harrison, *Lac de Garde*

AUTOMNE 1927, Roderic O'Connor, *Le pot chinois.*
AUTOMNE 1928, Edith Morgan, *Fleurs.*

As one can see, there is nothing exceptional in these purchases, French taste dominates and the understanding of the British artistic currents is almost non-existent. Léonce Bénédite who, otherwise, knew Edmund Davis and his collection well, shows considerable prudence and conservatism which do not fail to surprise us. On the whole the works are agreeable to look at and technically correct, but there seems to be very little inspiration in their choice. One should remark that for the year 1914 when, the noise of impending war increasing, France showed a certain liberality in buying five English paintings in the same year. If one sums up these purchases, only a few names stand out : Rupert Bunny is the major Australian artist of this period, Sir John Lavery was one of the great portraitists of his time, and lastly Roderic O'Connor, one of whose works was bought during the last years of the 1920s. It is certainly not a succession of masterpieces, nothing comparable to what was acquired from Americans like Whistler and Winslow Homer thus enabling the musée d'Orsay to be proud to possess at least one of their masterpieces.

This introduction, this essay, is certainly only a rapid overview, but it must be admitted that outside the period around the Salon of 1824, it is as yet difficult to establish a deeper review. Studies are in their infancy, they are scattered and sparse, sometimes even totally absent. This compilation of artists and works shown in the Paris Salons gives, for the first time, a continuous idea of one of the aspects of Franco-British relations. Numerous research projects are needed to diversify the surveys, the points of view, the facts, the analyses. One has, for the sole subject of the Salons themselves, to note the difference of nature between the Salons and the painting sections of the *Expositions Universelles.* These two sorts of manifestations have been brought together here for reasons of commodity for the future reader and not because that they were considered to be of the same nature. It is striking to note that the Salons do not show the same artists as the *Expositions Universelles.* The first are the result of a sum of individual initiatives whilst the second are manifestations run by the States concerned with their image abroad. Undeniably, the second are artistically richer and more representative of the artistic excellence of a country, undeniably also the first represent much better the ensemble of artists. Both one and the other bring to the scholar noteworthy material for study. One finds them brought together here for a better understanding of British painting.

Olivier Meslay

Conservateur au Musée du Louvre
(Translation by Geoffrey Cappner)

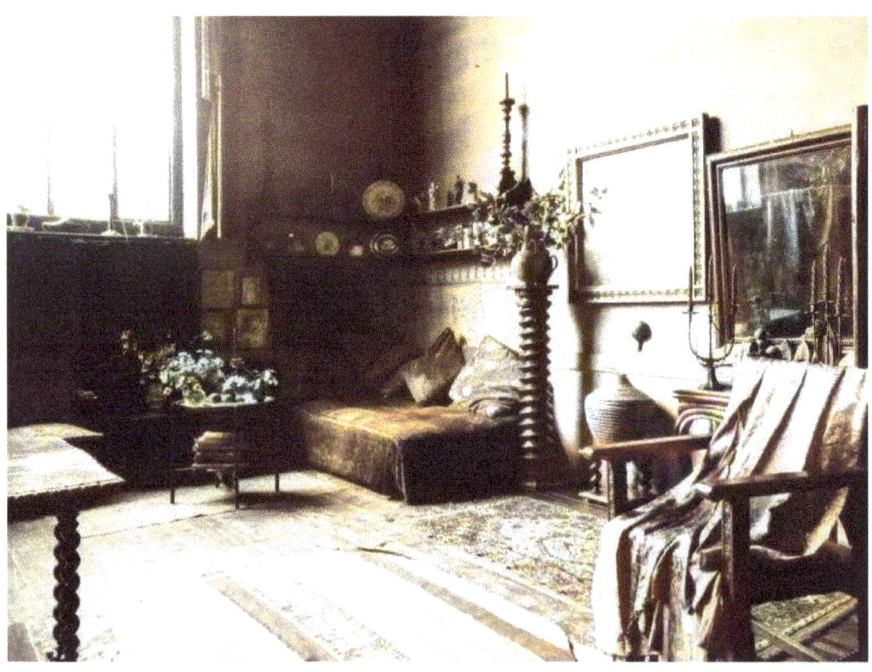

The studio of Hilda Rix Nicholas in Paris 1925.

www.ingramcontent.com/pod-product-compliance
Lightning Source LLC
LaVergne TN
LVHW052346100826
845147LV00012B/763
* 9 7 8 1 9 2 2 6 9 8 9 5 7 *